Fire Service Manual

Volume 2
Fire Service Operations

Incident Command

3rd Edition

2008

London: TSO

information & publishing solutions

Published by TSO (The Stationery Office) and available from:

Online
www.tsoshop.co.uk

Mail, Telephone, Fax & E-mail
TSO
PO Box 29, Norwich, NR3 1GN
Telephone orders/General enquiries: 0870 600 5522
Fax orders: 0870 600 5533
E-mail: customer.services@tso.co.uk
Textphone 0870 240 3701

TSO@Blackwell and other Accredited Agents

Customers can also order publications from:
TSO Ireland
16 Arthur Street, Belfast BT1 4GD
Tel 028 9023 8451 Fax 028 9023 5401

ISBN 978-0-11-341321-8   363.3781 STA

2nd impression 2009

Cover photograph courtesy of West Yorkshire Fire and Rescue Service
Printed in the United Kingdom for TSO

N6064854 C10 3/09

Contents

Chapter 1 – Fire and Rescue Service Incident Command Doctrine

1.1 The Incident Command System

The Incident Command System (ICS) constitutes the doctrine of the Fire and Rescue Service (FRS) in the context of operational incident management, leadership, and the functional command and control processes that flow from it.

The Incident Command System is the recognised "nationwide safe and effective system for managing operations".[1] It presents the key elements of effective incident command in three functional areas; these are:

- Organisation on the Incident Ground – this gives the Incident Commander a recognised system from which to work when organising and using resources at an Incident.
- Incident Risk Management – the principal consideration of Incident Commanders is the safety of their personnel. Therefore, prior to deciding upon the tactics an assessment of risk must be performed. The Incident Commander must identify the hazards, assess the risks, and implement all reasonable control measures before committing crews into a risk area.
- Command Competence – considers the skills knowledge and understanding required by an Incident Commander and the importance of maintaining such competencies.

Additionally, this edition of the manual reflects the need for FRSs to be able to work effectively within a broader multi-agency incident management framework. Building upon changes to legislation and supporting guidance[2] the broader role of Fire and Rescue Services in incidents other than fire is considered in relation to the capacities, objectives, and constraints of other responding agencies.

The Incident Command System and supporting processes described in the following chapters constitutes a template against which incident command policies and procedures can be written in FRSs, and the training and assessment of individuals and teams to operate those systems safely and effectively can be conducted. Any amendment to this template should be proposed to the Chief Fire and Rescue Adviser's Unit (CFRAU).

The Incident Command System itself operates within a wider framework of policies, values and an in depth understanding of operational issues which must be taken into account by staff in all roles in the FRS. Some of these are considered below.

1.2 Leadership

The Fire and Rescue Service in England and Wales has chosen to express its values and vision of leadership in the form of a simple model. The model has been named "Aspire". It has at its heart, the core values of the service; which are:

- Diversity
- Our People
- Improvement
- Service to the Community

---

1 Framework Document 2006-08

2 Fire and Rescue Services Act 2004, Civil Contingencies Act 2004, HM Government Emergency Response and Recovery (Non-statutory guidance document) and Emergency Preparedness (Statutory guidance do cument)

Although not usually discussed in the context of incident command, it can be seen that the values are intrinsic to everything we strive to achieve at an operational incident, where we routinely serve all of our communities equally and professionally, with the safety and well being of our own crews at the forefront of our mind and reflecting on how well we have done in order to be better next time.

The core values inform and underpin the personal qualities and attributes (PQAs) at each role level. Thereafter the model describes the "Leadership Capacities" and "Leadership Domains", which take the model a stage closer to the actual behaviours and outcomes:

Leadership Capacities:

- Organising and Changing
- Partnership Working
- Delivering Services
- Community Leadership
- Setting Direction
- Priorities and Resources
- Personal and Team Skills

These are practiced in the three Leadership Domains:

- Operational
- Political
- Personal-team approach

■ Core Values ■ PQAs ▨ Leadership Qualities ▨ Leadership Domains

Command and Control of operational incidents is inextricably linked with the Aspire model and the values of the Service. Operational incident command represents an area where leadership takes on a risk critical and central role. In recent years the Fire and Rescue Services has advanced the notion of leadership in many ways that appear to be allied to, but distinct from, the operational context. The identification of core values and the expression of key domains provide an excellent platform upon which to build a robust command and control doctrine. It is sometimes thought that such work is left behind when the "bells go down", and the service is called into action in its key operational intervention role. This is not the case. Perhaps the clearest example of the area where strong leadership and the ethic of the FRS comes into play is in the area of Dynamic Risk Assessment (DRA). The concept that "firefighters will take some risk to save saveable lives"[3] has to be professionally, ethically and effectively managed.

Leadership in the domain of critical incident command is often characterised by the need to deal with uncertainty in demanding timeframes. The role of the leader in such circumstances was described by Henry Kissinger, who stated that: "The most important role of a leader is to take on his shoulder the burden of ambiguity inherent in difficult choices. That accomplished, his subordinates have criteria and can turn to implementation". (Kissinger, 1982).

1.3 The Operational Environment

The Nature of Critical Incidents

The requirement to develop and apply an incident command system is driven by the critical nature of many of the incidents which the FRS responds to. These incidents often share common characteristics, including:

- Time sensitivity/ tempo of activity. Time pressure on the requirement to make decisions and act upon them is arguably the major contributory factor in the determination of incident criticality. Further to that, time pressure on decision-making will, by definition, drive the tempo of activity in any incident response.
- Complexity. Critical incidents may be accompanied by a degree of complexity that will result in uncertainty about outcomes.
- Moral Pressure. Critical incidents involving people and property at risk will generate moral pressure on those responding who may feel under pressure to quickly take action.
- Duty of Care. Closely related to the above characteristic will be the duty of care by those in command at critical incidents to avoid exposing their people to unnecessary exposure to risk.
- Retrospective Scrutiny. Those in positions of authority at critical incidents must expect to have their decisions and subsequent actions publicly scrutinised.

1.4 The Incident Command Environment

In general, incidents will generate an increasingly intense command environment as the complexity and scale increases. However, the commander must realise that intensity is also relative to the position and circumstances perceived by any individual involved in such an incident.

For example, a firefighter in breathing apparatus, operating in offensive mode at a dwelling fire in which persons are reported, will be subject to a more intense and narrowly focused experience of the incident than the officer outside the building in a position of command. Such an example can be developed through increasing layers of command present at complex larger scale incidents, further removing the overall incident commander from a

---

3 See 4.2 in this manual.

multitude of high-pressure situations. Therefore, a critical success factor in responding to any incident will be the commander's understanding of the whole context and the complete environment within which command is to be exercised.

Of the three Leadership Domains identified within the "Aspire" Leadership Model, incident command resides largely within the operational context. This assumption is more valid at operational levels of response. However, the reference above to the requirement for commanders to fully understand the incident command environment is of increasing relevance here. As the complexity/scale/intensity of incidents escalates, so too does the requirement for a broader understanding across the three Leadership Contexts. At the lower end, incident commanders will address, in the main, internal factors i.e. those confined largely to the incident ground. As the complexity, scale and intensity increases, the incident commander will be faced with a greater degree and frequency of issues regarding external FRS support, multi-agency considerations, as well as media, legal and political considerations. Therefore, the demands of the FRS Leadership Model directly reflect the demands of competent incident command throughout a successful FRS career at all levels.

1.5 Leadership in Operation

The Incident Command Policy Framework

The procedures that form the Incident Command System should be an integral part of a Fire and Rescue Service's organisational systems for managing risk. The approach published by the Health & Safety Executive in HSG65[4] provides an essential framework for designing and implementing organisational structures and processes for managing successfully and safely. HSG65 has five key elements which make up the framework.

1.5.1 Policy

There should be effective policies which set a clear direction for the organisation to follow, contributing to all aspects of business performance. Fire and Rescue Service's policies should set out the approach to delivering effective incident command. The model described in this manual provides a consistent approach that can ensure interoperability throughout the UK. Interoperability is critical both for routine cross border mutual aid operations and for larger scale incidents involving deployment of national assets, for example major emergencies requiring urban search and rescue or mass decontamination. Apparently minor modifications, for example a change in terminology, can cause confusion when fire and rescue services have to work together.

1.5.2 Organising

There needs to be an effective management structure and arrangements in place to deliver the policies. The arrangements should be underpinned by effective staff involvement and participation and be sustained by effective communication and promotion of competence. All involved should understand the Fire and Rescue Service's approach and objectives in relation to the command function, in particular the procedures associated with their area of responsibility.

---

4 HSG65 *Successful health and safety management* 2nd Edition ISBN 0 7176 1276 7

1.5.3 Planning

There should be a planned and systematic approach to implementing the policies through an effective management system. The aim is to deliver an effective response which minimises risks. Risk assessment techniques should be used to decide on priorities and set clear objectives for the incident response. Generally there is a hierarchy of control measures with preference being given to eliminating or controlling hazards rather than relying on systems of work or personal protective equipment. In the context of the Fire and Rescue Service operational incidents it is not always possible to eliminate hazards although this should be done by the selection and design of equipment and processes wherever possible. Risks should be minimised through appropriate physical controls or, where these are not possible, through systems of work and personal protective equipment.

1.5.4 Measuring performance

Performance should be measured against agreed standards to reveal when and where improvement is needed. Active self-monitoring reveals how effectively the management system is functioning, looking at equipment, processes and individual behaviour/performance. If the incident response is ineffective or health and safety controls fail, reactive monitoring discovers why, by both determining the immediate causes of the sub-standard performance and identifying the underlying causes, with the implications for the design and operation of the management system.

1.5.5 Auditing and reviewing performance

Fire and Rescue Services should learn from all relevant experience and apply these lessons. There needs to be a systematic review of incident command performance by Fire and Rescue Services based on monitoring data and independent audits of the management system. There should be both internal reference to key performance indicators and an external comparison with relevant best practice. There should be a strong commitment to continuous improvement in the delivery of the

Incident Command System, involving the constant development of policies, systems and techniques for delivering an effective and safe response.

1.6 The Incident Commander's Leadership Role

It is the duty of the Fire and Rescue Service Incident Commander at an operational incident to exercise authority over fire service resources on the incident ground.

The Incident Commander has much to consider when dealing with an emergency and the task will become more complex with increased scale and duration. Clearly, no officer can be expected to remember everything, so the system of incident command described in this manual will provide operational and managerial prompts to reinforce those given by the incident itself and the personnel in support roles.

The Incident Commander must ensure that adequate resources are available and that arrangements have been made to control them. At larger incidents these will normally be delegated as the responsibility of supporting officers in the command structure.

Good communication between personnel, on and off scene, is essential throughout the incident but especially at the time of the handing over of command, which can result in confusion if it is not done properly. The accumulated knowledge of the site, the incident, the risks and the actions taken so far need to be communicated, in an easily assimilated form, to the officer taking over.

An Incident Commander should be prepared to brief a more senior officer at any time so that a decision can be made whether or not to assume command. If the senior officer decides to take command then this intention must be made clear to the existing IC, by using some form of words such as "I am taking over". The change of command must also be relayed to Fire Control. Having assumed command the senior officer will in all likelihood want to retain the previous commander in the command structure to provide advice and continuity.

It is the duty of officers being relieved to give the officer who is assuming command all the relevant information they possess concerning the incident. Handover of command to more junior officers as the incident is being reduced in size must be equally thorough.

When taking over a command role on the incident ground, it is necessary to bear in mind the key elements of the role. It is essential to assume command at the appropriate time, according to either standard operating procedures or to the senior officer's judgement of how the incident is developing. Every effort should be made to avoid a 'time lag' during handover, where no one is focussed on making vital decisions due to the exchange of information at the handover. The new IC must make it clear that a single team is now operating under their leadership. Key elements of the leadership role are:

- the maintenance of shared situational awareness by effective communications;
- clear planning and setting of operational priorities;
- direction and focusing of activity in pursuit of objectives;
- ensuring subordinates have freedom and resources to carry out their role safely within the plan.

The following paragraphs illustrate the model of command and control used by the emergency responders in the UK. There are many cases where the roles may appear to overlap. This is to be expected, as the strength in a system lies in its flexibility and adaptability. Adapting the model to fit particular circumstances, based on a deep understanding of how the model would normally be applied is entirely different to failing to adhere to the model because of poor procedures, understanding or weak command. For example, whereas decision making levels are clearly defined, common sense dictates that where a tactical decision has to be taken by an officer of relatively junior rank in the absence of a senior officer, it will be taken. Equally, someone operating at tactical level will not overlook an urgent operational issue that arises that can easily be dealt with, merely on the grounds that it is not an appropriate task for their command level.

The FRS Incident Commander must focus on the safe and effective resolution of the incident, working at a tactical level, in conjunction with other services and agencies as necessary, to return circumstances to normality as soon as possible. In the UK emergency services context, tactics can be summarised as the deployment of personnel and equipment on the incident ground within set objectives and priorities to achieve the overall aims. The IC is therefore principally concerned with the tactical co-ordination of tasks in progress, which will be based on approved operational procedures.

Operations can best be described as tasks that are carried out on the incident ground to achieve desired objectives, using prescribed techniques and procedures in accordance with the tactical plan to achieve the strategic aims of Gold where that level of Command is in operation.

At the smaller incidents all decision making will be the responsibility of one individual (the IC), in conjunction with the Service's policies and procedures. This is likely to be the first arriving Crew Commander, who will be very much concerned with the tactics and operational tasks in the initial stages, delegating responsibility for the operational level if sufficient resources are available. At larger incidents the team of officers responsible for the various command functions will be organised by the Incident Commander to discharge the operational tasks, while the Incident Commander retains overall tactical command. Whereas it is highly unlikely that strategic decisions will have to be made at this level, if the need were to arise, the responsibility to deal with the issues at hand resides with the most senior officer available.

Therefore, at any incident, the Incident and/or Sector Commanders have a set of tactical priorities to follow. These can be found in Chapter 2.

1.7 Operating within the Multi-Agency Bronze, Silver and Gold Structure

Bronze, Silver and Gold, reflecting operations, tactics and strategy, are the descriptions given to the managerial levels of fire service involvement,

the first two being located on the incident ground. These terms need to be understood in the context of the incident command structure. This section of the manual describes the broad command and leadership remit of each level, with more detail about the functions and lines of communication being found in subsequent chapters.

In the following paragraphs, it must be borne in mind that most incidents are managed without the need for an elaborate structure. The vast majority of fires and Road Traffic Collisions (RTCs) are likely to be dealt with by crews being managed by their line supervisors. Even if an FRS incident escalates and more senior fire officers assume command, it should not be assumed that the multi-agency Bronze, Silver, Gold system will be applied. However, it is important to understand what the levels mean, and what functions they have responsibility for if the structure is implemented.

1.7.1 Operational (Bronze) Level Command

At the start of every incident for which there has been no warning, the 'operational level' will be activated first. The IC will attend the scene, (or as close as is deemed safe to do so depending upon the nature of the incident and resulting risk assessment). The role of the IC is to:

- Assess the extent of the incident, the number of resources, hazards and risks.
- Consider the appropriate level of command.
- Prioritise objectives.
- Develop and implement plan taking into account SOP and DRA.
- Communicate and control the plan.
- Evaluate the effectiveness of plan.

The findings of the above assessment will prompt the IC to consider whether to request additional resources should they be required, either in the form of specialist equipment or purely for additional personnel. Any such request at an incident may trigger the attendance of a more Senior Officer(s) and a dedicated Command Support Officer (Team).

If the incident becomes multi-agency and other services are operating their command structures at similar levels, then the FRS 'Incident Commander' would assume the role of 'Fire Silver'. Likewise, Sector Commanders would become 'Fire Bronzes'. Bronze Commanders must motivate and control crews doing difficult, dangerous, and sometimes distressing work. They frequently have to lead from the front. Consequently, their timeframes are typically short, with quick decisions and ongoing appraisals of the developing risks (Dynamic Risk Assessment) being necessary a lot of the time.

1.7.2 Tactical (Silver) Level Command

The Silver Commander's role is to manage the overall incident, determining priorities, allocating resources and obtaining additional resources as required. It will be necessary to plan and co-ordinate tasks to be undertaken and liaise with other agencies wherever necessary to co-ordinate efforts to achieve this. The Silver on-scene commander may also need to consider whether there is the need for a Gold or Strategic level of command if one is not already in place, and if so communicate this upwards.

A key task of the Silver Command function is to give early consideration to the 'consequence management' and recovery phases of the incident. This consideration may also suggest that a Gold Command would help to address such issues, leaving the tactical command to be undertaken from the scene.

Where there is an identifiable geographical focus of an incident, tactical management or Silver Command is usually undertaken from an Incident Control Point normally adjacent to the scene of operations. Other agencies however, may choose to discharge their functions from a remote location, i.e. the Police may adopt a Police Station for example or the Local Authority may chose to operate from their administrative offices. In such cases it is vitally important to co-operate through liaison officers who would provide a vital transfer of information. If the incident is geographically dispersed, such as wide area flooding, riot situations or perhaps the consequences of an air crash, the senior fire commander will make a decision about where the optimum location should be.

In a developing situation and where the use of either a significant additional resources or specialist equipment is required, the Silver Commander may be assisted by an FRS specialist advisor. These advisors are specialists in their particular fields and may be mobilised by the FRS National Co-ordination Centre (FRSNCC) to attend an incident to offer tactical advice to the IC. It is not intended that they take charge of any incident.

The value of an FRS advisor at a tactical level has been recognised because FRS officers cannot be expected to have a complete and detailed knowledge and understanding of every policy and procedure surrounding the diverse roles of Urban Search and Rescue (USAR), Mass Decontamination (MD), High Volume Pumping

(HVP) etc. When utilising resources provided by the New Dimension Programme (often referred to as "national assets") special provisions have become necessary. This includes a 'Convoy Procedure' for moving a number of vehicles, potentially over large distances throughout the country, a 'Strategic Holding Area' for holding the vehicles close to the scene of operations prior to deployment, and Enhanced Command Support (ECS) which will be adopted to support the existing command structure and assist in the control and co-ordination of these additional assets.

1.7.3 Strategic (Gold) Level Command

Most incidents, and the early stages of more serious incidents, may only require operational, or operational and tactical, levels of command. If it becomes apparent that the scale of resources or level of decision making required are beyond the tactical commander's capacity or authority, or if there is the need to co-ordinate more than one incident/ scene, then a Strategic or 'Gold' Command will be necessary. Gold will be a major support to Silver, often discussing tactics and their implications and acting as an advisor.

The strategic or "Gold" level is the most senior in an organisation and rarely comes into play in pure Fire Service operations. However, it can often feature in multi-service operations such as major incidents, large-scale civil disorder, wide area flooding or other protracted and serious incidents. Whereas "Gold" does not directly deal with operations on the ground, at tactical or "Silver" level, it can often involve political considerations and policy level decisions that extend beyond a single organisation. 'Gold' or strategic command is invariably exercised at a distance from the scene of the incident. It is intended to take the longer view of the situation; the time frame of Gold, or strategic command, is in days rather than hours or minutes.

Major incidents may place considerable demands on the resources of the responding organisations, with consequent disruption of day to day activities, and they may have long-term implications for a community or the environment. Such matters will need to be addressed strategically through Gold or the Strategic Co-ordinating Group (SCG) as it may be referred to, or possibly even the Regional Civil Contingencies Committee (RCCC), see Chapter 3.

SCG members are representatives drawn from all relevant agencies with the authority to make executive decisions appropriate to the circumstances.

The Gold Commander will typically:

- Be located away from the scene. Most agencies have dedicated facilities for such occurrences.
- Establish a framework for the overall management of the incident(s).
- Establish a policy within which Silver Commanders will work, also known as setting 'tactical parameters' an example of which may be 'allowing a fire to burn itself out' where 'run off water' could cause an environmental catastrophe as oppose to airborne pollution.
- Determine strategic objectives that should be recorded and periodically reviewed.
- Provide resources, or determine limitations upon levels of resourcing.
- Prioritise the demands from a number of Silver Commanders and allocation of resources.
- Ensure that there are clear lines of communication.
- Ensure that there is long term resourcing and expertise for command resilience.
- Undertake appropriate liaison with strategic managers in other agencies.
- Plan beyond the immediate response phase for recovering from the emergency and returning to a state of 'new normality'.

The requirement for strategic management may not apply to all responding agencies owing to different levels of engagement; however emergencies are invariably multi-agency and rarely remain with a single agency. It may therefore be appropriate for an agency not involved at strategic level to send a liaison officer to the meeting of the SCG. SCG members are representatives drawn from all relevant agencies with the authority to make executive decisions appropriate to the circumstances.

The SCG should be based at a pre-planned location, away from the noise and confusion of any disaster scene, normally in the first instance police headquarters. On most occasions it will be the responsibility of the police to establish and chair the group. However this may change to the 'lead' organisation, for example the local authority during the recovery phase when the emergency services have little or no involvement.

In the event of a wide scale emergency the SCG will need to liaise with neighbouring SCGs and in the recovery phase, the appropriate Government Office of the region or devolved administration.

A member of one of the Fire and Rescue Service's specialist advisory teams may be mobilised to advise the Fire Gold Commander at an incident which may be unusually large, protracted or "catastrophic".

1.8 The Operational Commander's Competence

Because of the widely differing demands of the various command and operational roles within major incident management, the competences associated with each level are necessarily different. Chapter 5 outlines this in more detail, and gives guidance to those responsible for development and assessment of commanders at key levels. The key levels are reflected in the National Occupational Standards (NOS), WM.7 for those working at the operational level of command and EFSM.2 for those responsible for tactical or incident ground levels of command. EFSM.1 describes the role of those tasked with supporting and leading incident management from a strategic perspective. Roles within the ICS will draw on those standards as appropriate, and some variations in application will necessarily be found, reflecting particular circumstances of the incident, the organisations involved, the capabilities of the command team, etc.

1.9 Incident Management and Decision Making

The processes associated with the management and command of serious or large scale operational incidents are complex and detailed. Much work has been done to assist Incident Commanders and others charged with operational responsibilities to understand the cognitive and emotional processes that occur at such times. Appendix 3 to this manual gives an insight into the psychological processes involved. Understanding these will help in dealing with ones own reactions to challenging situations as they arise.

However, such a description of the cognitive processes is not a tool. In the search for a device to practically assist commanders in the discharge of their responsibilities, experienced officers have reported the value they have derived from the Decision Making Model developed by the London Fire Brigade. See Figure 1 overleaf.

This is a cyclical process control model, not unlike a Deming "Plan, Do, Check, Action" cycle (Deming W E, "Out of the Crisis", Cambridge, Press Syndicate, 1982), which may assist commanders in achieving their operational objectives. An obvious application is in the analytical phase of the risk assessment. The full explanatory note is appended at Appendix 4, courtesy of London Fire Brigade.

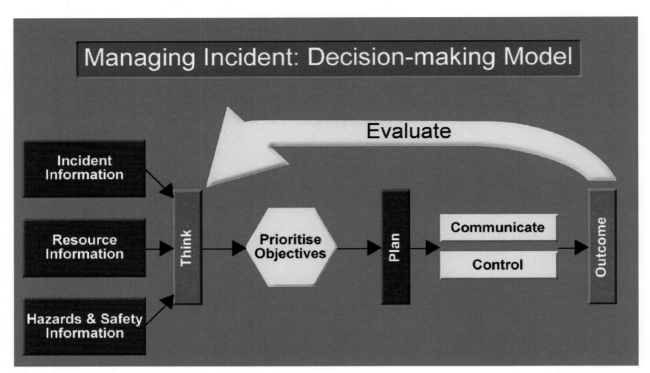

Figure 1

Chapter 2 – Organisation on the Incident Ground

2.1　General

This chapter focuses on organising and controlling operations on the incident ground, including the specialist support to operational sectors from support sectors and advisors.

The Incident Command System (ICS) provides a clear framework to assist the Incident Commander to organise and deploy available resources in a safe and efficient manner. It provides the IC with a ready to use organisational structure that can be adapted to fit every incident, from a one pump attendance to the largest most complex incident. It is therefore essential that the ICS is adopted in full and becomes familiar to all personnel so that the 'language' and concepts are fully understood

in readiness for not only localised incidents, but for cross border and national incidents of varying complexity.

2.2　The Role of the Incident Commander

The FRS Incident Commander at an operational incident is the 'nominated competent person', usually identified by wearing the IC's surcoat. This role need not invariably be fulfilled by the most senior officer present, but the senior officer present does have a moral and organisational responsibility within the overall command structure that cannot be divested. This arrangement allows an officer more senior to the IC to adopt a mentoring or monitoring role.

As each operational incident is different, IC's will need to adapt the strategic plans and systems of work, which are based on generic risk assessments, in the light of the specific circumstances of the incident, and the resources actually available to deal with those risks.

At any incident, the Incident and/or Sector Commanders (SCs) have to set tactical priorities. The following is an example of a typical list of objectives that have to be prioritised at a structure fire.

1. Perform rescues and ensure medical support is called for casualties without delay.
2. If the building is already fully involved in fire, take steps to prevent spread to exposure risks.
3. Contain the spread of fire within the building or affected portions of it as soon as possible.
4. Extinguish the fire.
5. Commence damage control operations as soon as conditions and resources allow.
6. Commence ventilation as soon as conditions and resources allow.
7. Commence cutting away and investigations to ensure all cavities and voids have been covered.
8. Consider the welfare of victims or those who have suffered loss at the earliest possible time, calling in external support as necessary.

This assumes an appropriate risk assessment has been completed, has been properly announced and is under continual review (see Chapter 4). These tactical priorities will also be helpful at debriefs and when ICs or Sector Commanders are self assessing their own, and their teams', performance at an incident:

The IC has much to consider when dealing with an incident and this will become even more complex with increased scale and duration. Clearly, no officer can be expected to handle every aspect of the operations in progress personally, so the system of incident command described in this manual will provide operational and managerial tools and support.

2.3 Levels of Command

There are three levels of command and control that may be brought into play at a multi-agency incident, known as Bronze, Silver and Gold. The terms are used to describe tiers of joint, multi-agency emergency management and will normally only be utilised where a combined multi-agency response is necessary. The adoption of this nationally agreed management framework will assist to integrate plans and procedures between agencies ensuring that roles and responsibilities are understood.

The UK's emergency responders model (Strategic – Gold, Tactical – Silver and Operational – Bronze), which is described in more detail in Chapter one, can be summarised as follows.

- **Operational** – which is the level at which command of immediate "hands-on" or task level work is undertaken at the scene of an incident. If the incident develops with several agencies needing to work effectively together, each sector would become a Bronze Command in line with other agencies. It must be emphasised that even if the incident is "multi-agency", the operational level role would not be formally labelled "Bronze" unless a tactical or silver level was in place, and usually when a multi-agency "Silver" group had been formed.
- **Tactical** – which is the level of overall command on the incident ground and which ensures that the Operational levels are supported, and if there are several sectors operating to ensure their operations are co-ordinated to achieve maximum effectiveness. Again, if the incident develops along multi-agency lines this role would become Silver Command. An incident may be formally structured with multi-agency Bronze and Silver Commands functioning without a 'Gold' being in place.
- **Strategic** – may be invoked where an event or situation may have significant impact on resources, probably involving a large number of agencies or has impact for an

extended duration. This will be referred to as Gold Command and will normally be implemented as a multi-agency group (SCG, see Chapter 3) bringing together Gold Commanders from relevant organisations. It is possible, but not usual, to designate a Gold Commander solely within an FRS operation of very large scale which is not impacting upon other organisations to any great extent. Whereas an incident may be structured up to Silver level without Gold necessarily being brought into play, if a Gold is formed, the levels below will invariably be structured as Silver(s) and Bronze(s).[5]

It should be borne in mind that different services, depending on the circumstances of the specific incident, may choose to exercise command at similar levels from different locations. The most common example of this is where the police Silver Commander chooses to locate in a police HQ or communications facility, whereas the FRS IC (or Fire Silver), chooses to co-ordinate the Fire Bronzes, or Sector Commanders, from the incident ground communications facility, most frequently a command unit. When the Fire Silver needs to attend a multi-agency liaison meeting at the police commander's HQ, or elsewhere, the incident ground will be left under the supervision of another senior member of the Silver Command team for the duration of the absence. In these circumstances, the designation of "IC" will rest with the officer on-scene.

If a fire incident, or multi-agency incident with a FRS controlled "hot zone", e.g. a USAR or mass decontamination event, escalates to Gold level, it is entirely possible that the Fire IC, who may be a Principal Officer, will assume incident command, sending a lower ranking officer, with the appropriate experience and authority to act, as the FRS representative at Gold. It is the responsibility of the Principal Officer to assume the Gold role as soon as circumstances permit. This reflects the positions are role related. It is, therefore, important for purposes of effective inter-service liaison that the levels of command and the labelling associated with them are understood but not interpreted too rigidly. Also, it needs to be understood that because an incident might be serious for one service, e.g., large fire for the fire service or a murder for the police, it does not necessarily involve other services, either at all, or at the same command level.

2.4 Duties of the Incident Commander at Operational (Bronze) Level

Upon arrival at an incident the IC has a wide base of information to consider and this will become even more complex and onerous as the incident escalates. It is therefore essential that consideration is given as soon as possible to start laying the foundations of the Incident Command System. This will include the following:

- Consider all of the relevant information, whether from the pre-planning stage or that available on the scene prior to forming a plan.
- Identify the hazards and risks to crews and third parties, and select a safe system of work ensuring that a 'Tactical Mode' is declared and communicated to all those on the incident ground and to central mobilising where it will be documented on your behalf.
- Assess the available resources against the objectives of the incident and request additional support where required.
- Form a robust plan to meet the objectives of the incident, prioritising where necessary if the resources are not adequate to achieve them simultaneously. The failure to prioritise may compromise a plan and put personnel at risk (see Decision Making Model in Chapter 1)
- Consider environmental issues such as run off water or airborne pollution as soon as practicable and where appropriate inform the relevant authorities, working within recognised protocols agreed with other agencies.

5 It should be borne in mind that the NATO hierarchy of Strategic, Operational and Tactical levels doesn't align directly to the structure of the UK Emergency Services, therefore allowances will have to be made where the military are deployed.

- Establish effective arrangements for communications, both on the incident ground itself and to provide regular updates to central control and oncoming supporting officers.
- Establish and maintain effective liaison with other agencies, whose knowledge may be critical in helping to achieve the objectives.
- Give early consideration to welfare, both of fire crews and any other party affected by the incident.
- Prepare to brief a more senior officer using all available relevant information so that a decision can be made as to whether that officer should assume command.
- Establish support in order to provide a reporting and holding area for oncoming resources, to assist with communications from the incident ground and to document necessary information, this will be formally referred to as Command Support.
- Constantly update the risk assessment and subsequent plan based on the availability of additional information.
- Communicate plan to Sector Commanders and ensure regular updates are given and received on progress.

2.5 Duties of the IC at Tactical (Silver) Level

On arrival at an incident the Tactical officer must report to Command Support and book in attendance, ensuring that mobilising control is made aware. Contact must be made with the IC as soon as practicable and the exchange of relevant information regarding the incident undertaken. A decision whether to take over the incident, remain at the incident in a mentoring or monitoring role, or allow the existing IC to remain in charge, must be taken and effectively communicated to all relevant parties. To ensure that there is no doubt about the 'handover', the process would be confirmed by the exchange of the IC's tabard.

Where the decision to take over the incident is undertaken, the following points must be considered:

- Confirm the existing plan according to the agreed tactical priorities.
- Confirm the risk assessment and Tactical Mode, ensuring that safe systems of work are being utilised.
- Ensure that the requested resources are adequate and effectively deployed to reflect the tactical priorities. If the incident is under resourced a request for further assistance should be made.
- Ensure that communications are effective and well structured informative messages have been passed on and documented.
- Review the command structure of the incident and ensure that no one is fulfilling a role beyond their experience and capability and that the spans of control of individuals remain manageable.
- Evaluate the tactical plan against all available information, ensuring that a risk v benefit analysis is performed (see Chapter 4).
- Confirm that adequate measures have been taken to address any welfare issues that may arise from the incident.
- Maintain effective liaison with other agencies ensuring that each are working towards a common set of objectives.
- Initiate any necessary investigations as soon as practicable, ensuring that possible evidence is recovered or preserved and witness statements are taken. Where legal proceedings may follow the police should be involved in the operational decision making process at the earliest possible time and full co-operation afforded to them.
- Consider any relevant points that would be of benefit during the debrief, including good and bad practices, success or failure of equipment or policies and the performance of crews.

The IC is responsible for securing and controlling resources on the incident ground. The assessment of resources will include consideration of the need for additional:

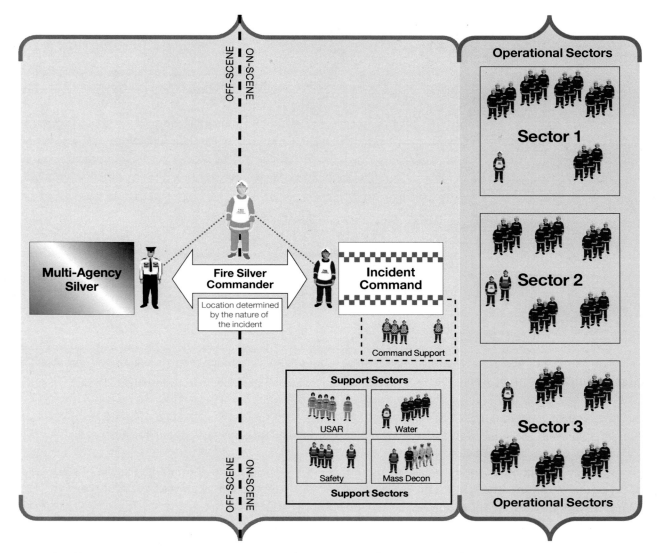

- Appliances
- Personnel
- Equipment
- Firefighting media
- Consumables (e.g. fuel, BA cylinders)

The degree of control an IC will need to maintain will depend, in part, on the size and demands of the incident. At larger incidents specific areas of resource control may be delegated to appointed officers. Such areas may include:

- Operational Sectors
- Command support
- Marshalling
- BA Main Control
- Logistics

- Decontamination
- Water
- Foam
- Relief Management
- Crew Rehabilitation and Welfare
- Safety
- Communications
- Press Liaison

Each of these functions may be assigned by the IC to support sectors if the scale of the operation demands it. If this occurs, the support Sector Commander will report in the line of command to the Command Support Officer, who has a similar command responsibility level to an Operations Commander (see Chapter 2.11.2).

Where complex or technical operations such as High Volume Pumping, Mass Decontamination or Urban Search and Rescue are being carried out in operational sectors, they can be assisted by support sectors in the same way as BA operations are supported by a BA Main Control. The IC must ensure that there is never any misunderstanding or confusion about the Incident or Sector Commander's direct line of operational command as opposed to the support and advice provided by support sectors and their staff, some of which may hold rank higher than those in the sectors being supported. It is important that mutual assistance arrangements and standard operating procedures fully address these issues.

2.6 Duties of a Strategic (Gold) Level Commander

This paragraph refers to the role of the senior FRS officer who will discharge the responsibilities of a strategic commander when a multi-agency Strategic Co-ordinating Group (SCG) is brought into play during an operational incident. The task is to take overall organisational responsibility for the management of that incident and to establish the policy and strategic framework within which Silver(s) will work. It is not intended that the Fire

Gold Commander will direct or take charge of operations on the actual incident ground. The Fire Gold Commander will participate in the multi-agency Gold group where one has been deemed appropriate, and from that position:

- Determine and promulgate a set of strategic aims and objectives and review them regularly.
- Set tactical parameters for Silver to operate within.
- Prioritise the demands of the Silver Commander(s) and allocate personnel and resources to meet requirements.
- Formulate and implement media handling and communication with the public.
- Direct planning and operations beyond the immediate response in order to facilitate recovery.
- Support and advise Silver.
- Work with partner agencies.

2.7 Structuring an Incident

The ICS is based on a framework that assists with the management of resources at an incident. It enables the IC to delegate responsibility for a range of tasks and functions during what may be a stressful, rapidly developing situation whilst remaining very much in control. The main elements of the standard ICS framework are:

- A clear, defined and visible line of command;
- Management of the span of control of key commanders;
- Appropriately shared responsibility and authority, with a clear definition and understanding of roles and responsibilities.
- A consistent and predictable pattern of sectorisation e.g. at a four sided building the front or main scene of operations becomes Sector 1, and Sectors 2, 3 and 4 are allocated in a clockwise rotation, Sector 3 being the rear. In unusual buildings or sites the IC should sectorise in a way as consistent with the model as possible

Understanding the concept of 'Span of Control' is key to managing large volumes of activity and information and is discussed more fully in 2.10, however, sectorisation is key to managing these volumes of activity and providing a clear line of reporting for everyone on the incident ground. Research has shown that at large incidents, ICs were not only making decisions about tactics, resources, logistics etc, but also mentally building an organisational chart at the same time. The use of a standard and predictable model of incident organisation, to be applied during the early stages of escalation, eases this task considerably. However it must be done correctly and consistently.

Adherence to common terminology is also very important as an aid to developing a common understanding of the situation which is being dealt with. The ICS uses 'roles' to describe responsibilities thus allowing individual FRSs to assign each function according to their own particular circumstances. The standard model allows the structure of the incident to develop in a predictable and manageable way.

2.7.1 Sectorisation of Incidents

Incidents are best managed if they are kept as simple as possible, if it is not necessary to sectorise, then to reduce the possibility of barriers to information flow between crews and the IC, it is best not to.

Sectorisation should be introduced when the demands placed upon an IC make it imperative that responsibility and authority are delegated to ensure appropriate command and safety monitoring of all activities, and to reduce officers' spans of control. Even if it is possible for the IC to oversee all operations, the need to sectorise will arise if there is so much going on that the IC risks being distracted and unable to give sufficient attention to each task. This would indicate that the IC's span of control is in danger of becoming too great. Where spans of control begin to reach or exceed 5 lines of direct communication at a working incident, it is possible that performance will be adversely affected.

The creation of sectors will only be done on the instructions of the IC who will sectorise appropriately to meet the demands of the incident following the standard model. Other than in exceptional circumstances, sectorisation must follow this standard model. Using this approach, Sector 1 is invariably located at the front (or main scene of operations) progressing thereafter in a clockwise direction, with Sector 3 normally at the rear. (see examples in the following diagrams). This will ensure continuity at major or cross border incidents where crews from two or more Fire and Rescue Services would likely attend.

In buildings or environments that don't lend themselves to the 'preferred model', then it is vitally important when delegating the responsibility of sectors that a thorough understanding of both the physical boundary and parameters in which to operate are communicated to all who need to understand the layout to avoid confusion.

Frequently, operations take place in more than one location during an incident, for example at the front and rear of a building. In such cases the IC's span of control may only be small. At a typical semi-detached house fire the IC has the ability to monitor tasks at front and back simply by moving to and fro, and therefore it is unlikely that there will be a need to sectorise. However, if the house is mid terrace with no quick access from front to rear, then despite the small span of control it is unlikely that the IC will be able to adequately manage operations and

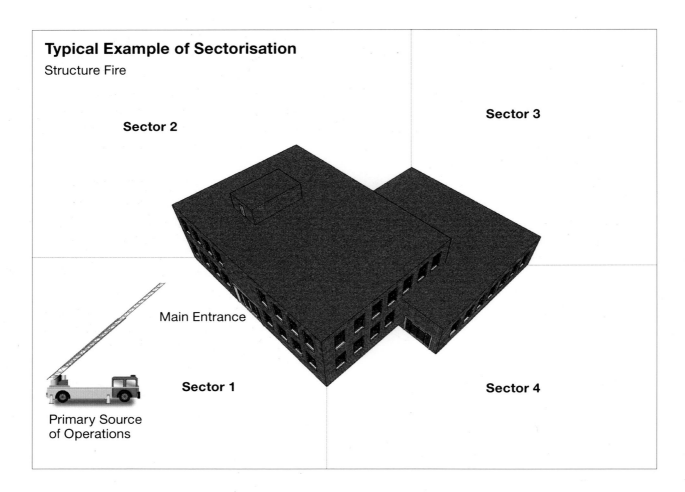

Typical Example of Sectorisation
Structure Fire

Sector 2

Sector 3

Main Entrance

Sector 1

Sector 4

Primary Source
of Operations

supervise safety at both locations simultaneously. In this case the most appropriate response would be for the IC to retain command of the front of the building, and to assign all operations at the rear of the building to another officer of appropriate level and experience.

It is important to note that where this happens at small scale incidents only, it is not mandatory that this officer is nominated as a Sector Commander and equally does not necessarily mean that a separate Sector Commander has also to be created for the front of the building.

Similarly, at an RTC there may be no need to formally sectorise, however if crews are assigned to a vehicle, which has come to rest 30 metres down an embankment remote from the main scene of operations on the roadway, it may be necessary to assign that vehicle as a separate area of responsibility, which might be a Sector.

The principle to be borne in mind is that sectorisation is driven by the need to delegate responsibility and authority in order to ensure appropriate command and safety monitoring of all activities.

2.7.2   Vertical Sectorisation
In buildings or structures with multi-floors where operations may be spread over several levels, i.e. high rise buildings or ships, the suggested model above would not prove to be effective or easy to execute. The vertical sectorisation model is based on maintaining effective spans of control when Sector Commanders cannot follow the normal practice of being physically present in the sector, due to smoke, heat etc.

At an incident in a multi-storey building external sectorisation may be necessary as well as internal, for example if aerial appliances are being used for access or rescue. External sectorisation would follow the normal model, identifying the sectors by number.

Internal sectorisation has to recognise the particular constraints of operating in an environment where the "fire floor" constitutes a barrier to the areas above, and to some extent the entire area from above the bridgehead, which is conventionally located two floors beneath the fire floor, must be considered a hazard zone. It may only be necessary to operate a single operational sector internally, with external and support sectors operating outside as described above. However, at an incident where a large number of personnel are firefighting, searching, or ventilating etc. more than one internal sector may be required to ensure that the Sector Commander's span of control is not exceeded. The zones of activity within the structure (e.g. internal firefighting operations) could then be identified as in the following examples:

- Fire Sector – this is an operational sector and would be the main area of firefighting and rescue operations, consisting of the floor/s directly involved in fire, plus one level above and one level below. If crews involved in this exceed acceptable spans of control, consideration should be given to activating a Search Sector..

- Search Sector – this is an operational sector and would be the area of operations in a high rise, above the 'fire sector' where search and rescue, venting and other operations are taking place. In a basement scenario the Search Sector could extend from fresh air to the lowest level. If the distance from the ground floor lobby to the bridgehead is more than two or three floors and spans of control require it, consideration should be given to activating a Lobby Sector.

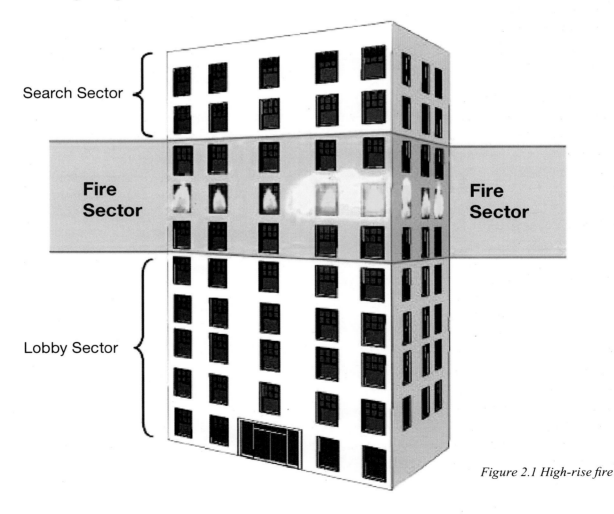

Figure 2.1 High-rise fire

- Lobby Sector – this is a support sector and would cover the area of operations from the ground floor lobby to the bridgehead, which is normally two floors below the fire floor. The Lobby Sector Commander will act as the co-ordinator of all the logistics needs of the fire and search Sector Commanders, who will, on most occasions, need to be located at the bridgehead directing operations via radio and liaising with the BAECO's. The Lobby Sector Commander would also co-ordinate all operations beneath the bridgehead level, including salvage and ventilation, liaising with fellow Sector Commanders in the usual way.

It is not intended that the system be over-prescriptive and situations may arise where other approaches may need to be taken, for example in a large or complex building it may be necessary to introduce more than one sector on a floor. This system was necessary at an actual incident, where two sectors were required each with its own bridgehead, operating in different stairwells and an Operations Commander co-ordinating the sectors from the lobby area.

All other aspects of the structure, e.g. lines of responsibility, lines of communication and reporting for the Sector Commander would function in the normal manner. See figure 2.1 for an example of vertical sectorisation.

These principles can be readily applied to other situations where vertical, internal sectorisation may be necessary.

The diagrams on p37–p43 are examples of the Incident Command structure applied to incidents, and how the command structure expands to match the demands of an escalating incident.

The layout is not intended to be prescriptive, but certain features are considered "standard". For example, external operational sectors are generally numbered not named. All operational sectors report direct to the IC or to the Operations Commander if one is in place.

All support sectors must report to the IC via the command support function. This is important to preserve spans of control. At more serious incidents, it is likely that the command support function will be headed by an officer of some seniority and experience.

Although the diagrams give examples of five, eight, fifteen etc, pump incidents, this is illustrative only and the range is, of course, variable and dependent on the requirements of the incident and the resources of the individual FRS.

Services and organisations listed to the right of the command support function, police and press, etc., (40 pump incident, p43) are examples only, and the list is far from exhaustive. It may include any or all of the agencies that are stakeholders in the incident.

The larger number of crew members in the vicinity of Command Support that appear in the diagrams after a command unit is in place, represent those allocated as command support and radio operators etc. Individual FRSs will have different ways of managing this requirement.

2.7.3   Location of Sector Commanders
It must be emphasised that Sector Commanders should be in direct communication with personnel in their sector. Sector Commanders provide direct and visible leadership at each sector and need to remain directly accessible to the Crew Commanders for whom they are responsible. In cases where it is essential that an IC requires a Sector Commander to leave their post, for a briefing or another purpose, they must be replaced by someone with appropriate competence and authority to maintain continuity of supervision. Any such replacement must be communicated to all those operating in the sector.

2.7.4   Support or Functional Sectors
Not only may incidents be sectorised geographically as described above, but they may be sectorised by 'function' or support sectors, e.g. water, decontamination etc, such sectors are designated as the IC sees fit and may be grouped according to availability of officers and resources to suit the need.

It is important that established lines of command are observed, Commanders of support sectors should report directly to Command Support.

Examples of support sectors include:

- Command Support
- Marshalling
- Logistics
- Safety
- Communication
- Water
- Foam
- Decontamination
- BA Main Control
- Welfare

2.7.5 Assuming and Handing-over Command of Sectors

When command of an incident changes for what ever reason it must be done in a disciplined and formal manner. This includes the appointment of, or change of a Sector Commander. In every case a clear and precise exchange of information must be undertaken to confirm the status of the incident or sector prior to assuming command or delegating responsibility.

2.8 Managing Crews on the Incident Ground

Where possible, crews should be kept intact and work as a team on the incident ground. An IC should remember that, for a variety of reasons, crews can be tempted to self-deploy. This must be avoided as it is essential to account for all of the available resources. A thorough briefing of crews must take place prior to deployment so that safety critical information can be shared. The main priority of any Incident Commander is the safety of personnel under their control. This must be established by identifying the risks that are present, adopting appropriate control measures and ensuring that safe systems of work are used. Using this approach firefighters can carry out their duties and remain safe whilst doing so.

At large and sectorised incidents in particular, it is important for crews to be aware of the IC's intentions and the overall objectives which have been set for the incident. This will form the parameters within which they are deployed in their sectors and crews.

Once crews have been briefed they must follow those requirements and work safely. This will include wearing the appropriate personal protective equipment (PPE) and ensuring that access and egress is properly secured at all times. The IC and Sector Commanders where appropriate will need to maintain a position where, as far as practicable, progress can be monitored. Where the level of risk requires it, the appointment of one or more safety officers must be considered to act as advisors at key levels.

Once crews are at work they will require a level of supervision and support, this may mean having the necessary resources available (e.g. BA cylinders and servicing facilities etc) and to ensure that their welfare needs are addressed. Care must be taken to give crews sufficient rest, relief and refreshment. The frequency of relief's will depend upon the demands of the incident and the individual policies of each FRS. A recognised problem exists at protracted rescues where personal commitment to the victims is high. Under these circumstances the level of fatigue must be measured against the continued desire to work. A balance must be found between safe operations and crew morale.

The potential for post-incident stress must be recognised and officers should be trained to identify signs of this. At protracted and complex incidents support and counselling may need to begin on the incident ground and must in any case be addressed as a post-incident consideration.

2.9 Line of Command

For the ICS to work effectively it is essential that all of those involved at each incident:

- are adequately trained,
- are competent,
- are confident in their ability,
- know who they are responsible for,
- know who they need to report to,
- know what their operational brief is.

The system provides for a line (or chain) of command to form to ensure that every activity on the incident ground, be it within a crew or a sector, is working under the responsibility of a competent person. The system must be flexible enough to meet the demands of every incident regardless of size or complexity, however, these principles are central to the system.

2.10 Span of Control

One facet of the span of control is the pivotal need to maintain lines of communications, which at times may be numerous, in order to achieve the objectives of the incident. This may consist of direct or indirect reports from individuals, crews or sectors.

Communications will also be received from other emergency services, assisting agencies and control centres. When analysing the span of control, careful consideration should be given as to how communications will be managed, and the pressures that may be placed upon the Incident Commander.

The system requires that direct lines of communication and areas of involvement need to be limited to manageable levels to enable the commander to cope with the flow of information. Failure to do so could, and indeed often does, result in essential, risk critical information being badly communicated or overlooked, the result of which could be catastrophic.

The span of control for tactical roles should ideally be as narrow as possible. No individual should be responsible for so many aspects of the incident that it is difficult or impossible to give sufficient attention to each. In most cases the span of control should be limited to five lines of direct communications, however this may in some cases be excessive depending upon the intensity of activity of those lines. Where this is apparent, for example during the fast moving early stages of an incident, the direct lines may need to be reduced or limited further to ensure that commanders do not become overburdened. In a rapidly developing or complex incident where the intensity is great, the span of control may need to be as small as 2 to 3, whereas later on, in more a stable situation, up to 6 or 7 may be acceptable.

The span of control for support roles, e.g. the Command Support Officer, may in some circumstances be wider, however this depends very much on the circumstances of the case and the stage of the incident.

Therefore the ICS offers a structure within which an appropriate span of control can be maintained at all times by providing for additional roles to be introduced into the incident command structure when the demands on any individual's attention become excessive.

At small incidents where the area of operations is easily manageable and the use of sectors not required, the IC may oversee all aspects of the incident directly. As the number of crews increases beyond 4 or 5, and the burden of supervision becomes more challenging, the IC should consider stepping back and appointing two or more Sector Commanders to supervise the crews. If the number of sectors has to increase beyond 4 or 5, the IC may choose to appoint an Operations Commander

to supervise the sectors. Likewise, if the number of sectors continues to grow, the IC may need to group the sectors under more than one Operations Commander. Naturally, incidents on such a scale are rare, nevertheless the system must be able to cope with them, and commanders must understand clearly how such a scale is dealt with by proper application of the standard ICS model.

In the diagram on page 34, an IC is responsible for 3 working crews at an incident and has detailed a firefighter to carry out a specific task, possibly Command Support, which involves regular contact. The span of control for this IC is 4.

2.11 Roles and Responsibilities within Incident Command

In order to manage a large incident effectively the IC may decide to delegate responsibility and devolve authority for some of the operations. This can be achieved by sectorising the incident, either geographically or by functions as described in Paragraph 2.7.4.

The Incident Commander remains at all times responsible for the overall management of the incident and will focus on the command and control, deployment of resources, tactical planning and co-ordination of the sector operations and running the incident itself.

2.11.1 Sector Commander

The Sector Commander will report to the IC or to the Operations Commander if one is in place, taking responsibility for the resources and the achievement of operational objectives within that sector. The Sector Commander will principally focus on command and control, deployment of resources, tactical planning, BA search co-ordination and most importantly health and safety of personnel. The progress of operations in each sector must be communicated fully to the Incident or Operations Commander to enable them to monitor the overall progress towards resolution of the incident. A Sector Commander has a high degree of operational independence in determining how the

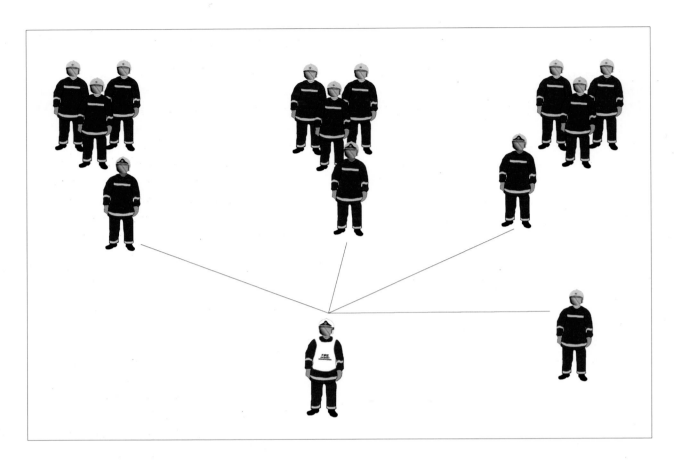

objectives agreed with the IC are to be delivered, but must at all times ensure that the IC is aware of the tactical mode being employed. Any change in tactics must have the IC's explicit approval, (or the approval of the operations commander where one is appointed), other than to withdraw personnel immediately from a potentially hazardous area. In such a case the IC must be informed as soon as is practicable and the tactical mode should be updated accordingly. The officer assigned to command of a sector must assume the incident ground radio call sign for that sector e.g. Sector Two Commander, sometimes just shortened to "Sector Two".

2.11.2 Operations Commander

The purpose of the Operations Commander is to allow the IC to maintain a workable span of control when an incident develops in size or complexity. If, for example, an incident has more than four operational sectors and some support or functional sectors such as water, decontamination, and damage control for example, then taking into consideration the likelihood that the IC would need to liaise with

the press, police, public and other agencies, the number of lines of communication will potentially become unmanageable.

The function of the Operations Commander is to supervise and co-ordinate the operations within sectors. The Operations Commander will also assume the responsibility on behalf of the IC of approving changes of tactical mode. The Operations Commander is a member of the command team and operates on behalf of the IC at Tactical/Silver level.

The Operations Commander should avoid becoming involved in support activities or dealing with the press etc, these functions being addressed by Command Support. This allows the Operations Commander to co-ordinate the Sector Commanders, offering support, addressing resourcing issues, and ensuring that risk assessments have been performed at the proper times, are of the expected quality, and have been appropriately recorded.

It is important to note that if an incident does not demand the use of an Operations Commander due to the number of sectors, or the activity within the sectors, then this extra tier is best omitted from the command structure. There is no advantage in over structuring an incident with additional tiers if they are not needed.

In the event that an incident requires more than one Operations Commander to maintain the span of control then it is essential to ensure that their call signs are suitably distinguishable, either by descriptive terms i.e. High Street Operations, Quayside Operations etc. or by alphanumeric terms i.e. Alpha Operations, Bravo Operations etc., and that sectors understand exactly which operations command they fall within and are reporting to. If the facility exists, consideration should be given to allocating different fireground or tactical radio channels to each operations command, e.g. sectors 1 to 4 on one channel reporting to Alpha Operations, sectors 5 to 8 reporting to Bravo Operations on a separate radio channel.

2.11.3 Command Support

Command Support should be introduced at all incidents to assist the IC in the management of the scene. It should be initiated as soon as is practically possible as the importance of laying the foundations of command support in the early stages of an incident cannot be over emphasised. A suitably experienced member of personnel should be nominated to operate Command Support. This may be a firefighter during the early stages operating in, or adjacent to an appliance at a smaller incident. The task being delegated to a suitably trained and experienced officer as an incident develops and more resources become available. The function may be managed from an appliance not directly involved in operations, an officer's car or a dedicated command vehicle of some kind. Command Support should be clearly identified at every incident.

Other responsibilities of Command Support include:

- To act as first contact point for all attending appliances and officers and to maintain a physical record of resources in attendance at the incident.
- To operate the main-scheme radio link to the mobilising control, to allocate fire ground radio channels and to log all relevant data.
- To assist the IC in liaison with other agencies, where appropriate a dedicated Liaison Officer may be appointed.
- To direct all resources to the required operational location or marshalling area as instructed by the IC and to record their operational status.
- To maintain a record of the findings of the risk assessment and operational decisions made or actions taken as a result of it.
- To allocate and record specific roles and assignments of supporting officers.
- To record information about sectors, such as the name of the Sector Commander, the identification of each sector, the physical boundaries where appropriate, the resources deployed and requested and the Tactical Mode in operation.

To assist with the function of the 'initial' command support duties, a support pack should be provided on all vehicles that may warrant its use.

At larger incidents where a dedicated Command Support vehicle is mobilised an officer should be delegated the task of heading the Command Support team (or Sector), with the task of supporting the IC.

Also at larger or escalating incidents, command support, which at this time may have become the Command Support Sector, may also be responsible for the following duties:

- To arrange the positioning of appliances and to some extent marshalling. This may need to become a specific function assigned to a dedicated support sector. Close liaison

with the police or Highways Agency Traffic Officers may be required to keep congestion to a minimum.

- Liaising with crews of specialist units such as BA Main Control, Urban Search and Rescue and High Volume Pumping etc. to ensure that they are utilised fully in support of the incident.
- Arranging for additional resources or specialist equipment as requested by the IC, in support of Sector Commanders.
- Liaising with other agencies as necessary, when such agencies attend an incident a system of 'logging' personnel must be implemented, especially if they are to enter the inner cordon. Supervision for such personnel may need to be arranged and a safety brief delivered prior to their deployment.
- Briefing designated personnel of their tasks and safety critical information.
- Arranging for relief crews and equipment to ensure sustainability of deployment.

- Mapping the progress of the incident.
- Logging decisions made and the rationale behind them.
- Constructing time lines and utilising them to prompt the IC regarding progress.

The amount of activity and span of control within the Command Support Sector must itself be continually monitored and where required additional staff should be requested to support the function.

2.11.4 The Command Team

The command team comprises of the IC and any other staff that are operating in a supporting role i.e. Command Support, Operations Commander and despite the likelihood of working from a remote location, Sector Commanders.

At incidents requiring specialist equipment i.e. USAR, HVP or Mass Decontamination etc, a specialist advisor may be deployed to assist the IC, in an advisory capacity only.

FRS's will almost certainly adopt different approaches to which roles and functions form part of the command team, however the aim is to integrate and record decision making and communication between the IC and those performing operational tasks. Some of the command support functions may take place from a location remote from the incident, particularly at major or multi-agency incidents.

2.12 Identification of Command Roles

The command team comprises officers holding a variety of roles and it is essential for each to be easily identified. At any incident, but in particular at cross border and other large incidents where officers who may not know each other personally have to work together, it is important that a commonly understood means of identification of roles is used. The following means of identification are not part of any standard but are in common usage:

 Incident Commander – White surcoat (or in Scotland, red and white quadrants)

 Sector Commander – Yellow surcoat with red shoulders

 Operations Commander – Red surcoat

 Command support – Red and white chequered surcoat

Efforts have been made to avoid patterns and colours used by other agencies wherever possible, but in the absence of a national multi-agency policy of identification it may be necessary to clarify roles at the time. It should be noted that the above patterns are for use at conventional incidents and the patterns described do not conflict with other task specific requirements for use on motorways, railways, airports etc. Common sense indicates, however, that a full command structure is unlikely to be established on a motorway carriageway or a railway embankment with live traffic.

In addition to the above the following are patterns of uniform that appear in the forthcoming diagrams and are for illustration purposes only.

Incident
Commander

Operations
Commander

Sector
Commander

Safety
Officer

Gas Tight
Suit Wearer

Mass Decontamination
Director/Assistant

Crew
Commander

USAR
Team Leader

USAR
Team Member

Crew
Member

BA Entry
Control Officer

Command Support
Officer

Sector
Boundary

Support Area

Key for the following diagrams

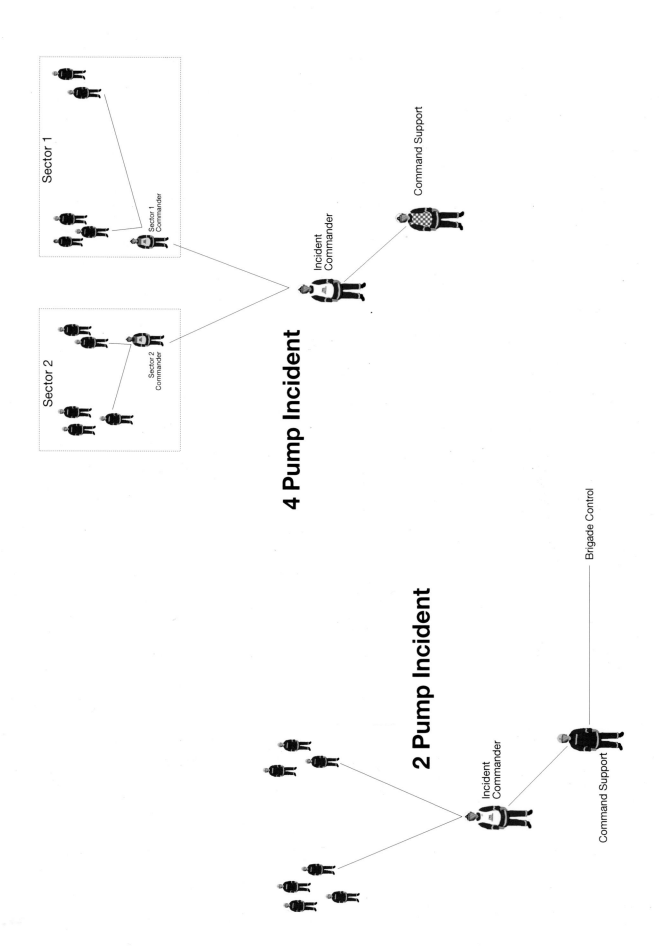

4 Pump Incident

Sector 1

Sector 1
Commander

Sector 2

Sector 2
Commander

Incident
Commander

Command Support

2 Pump Incident

Incident
Commander

Command Support

Brigade Control

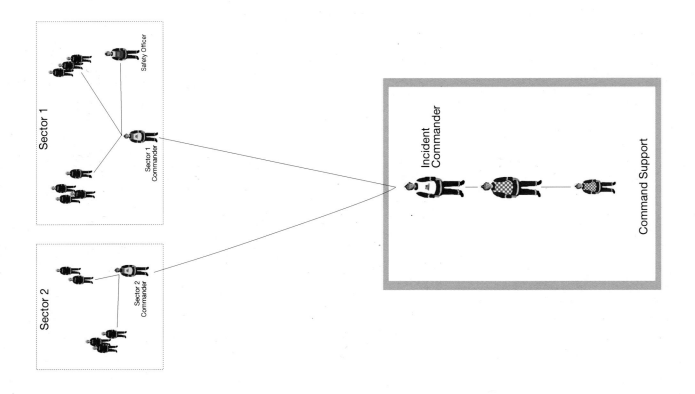

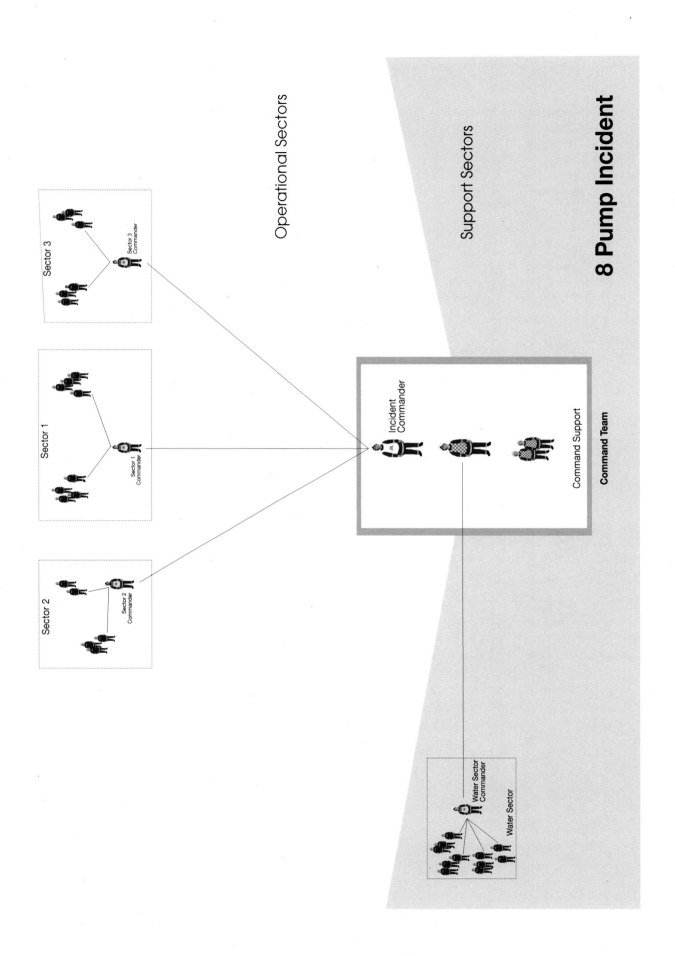

Operational Sectors

Sector 3

Sector 3
Commander

Sector 1

Sector 1
Commander

Sector 2

Sector 2
Commander

Support Sectors

Incident
Commander

Command Support

Command Team

Water Sector
Commander

Water Sector

8 Pump Incident

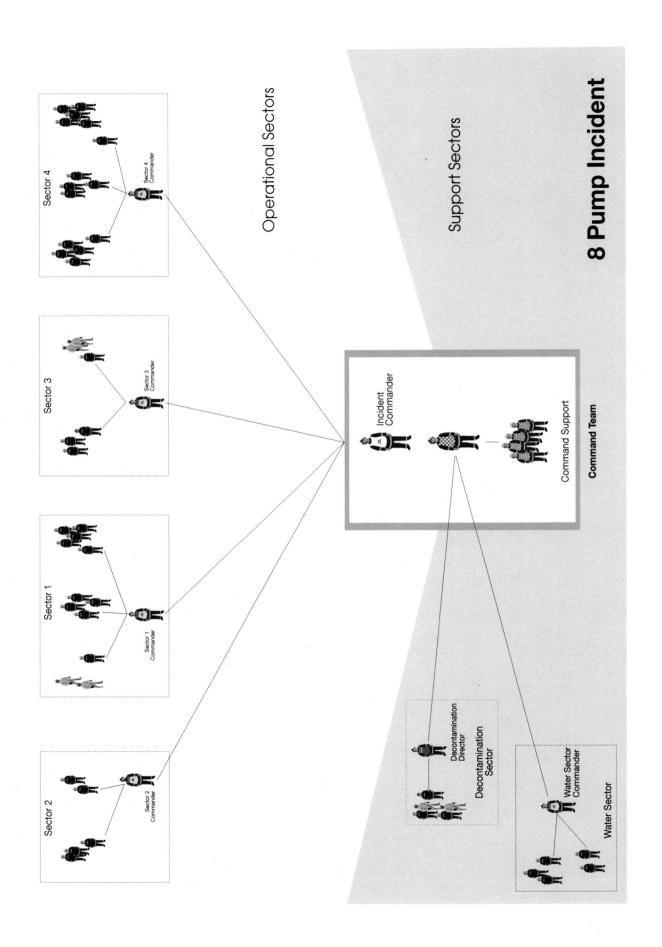

8 Pump Incident

Operational Sectors

Sector 4 — Sector 4 Commander

Sector 3 — Sector 3 Commander

Sector 1 — Sector 1 Commander

Sector 2 — Sector 2 Commander

Support Sectors

Incident Commander

Command Support

Command Team

Decontamination Director

Decontamination Sector

Water Sector Commander

Water Sector

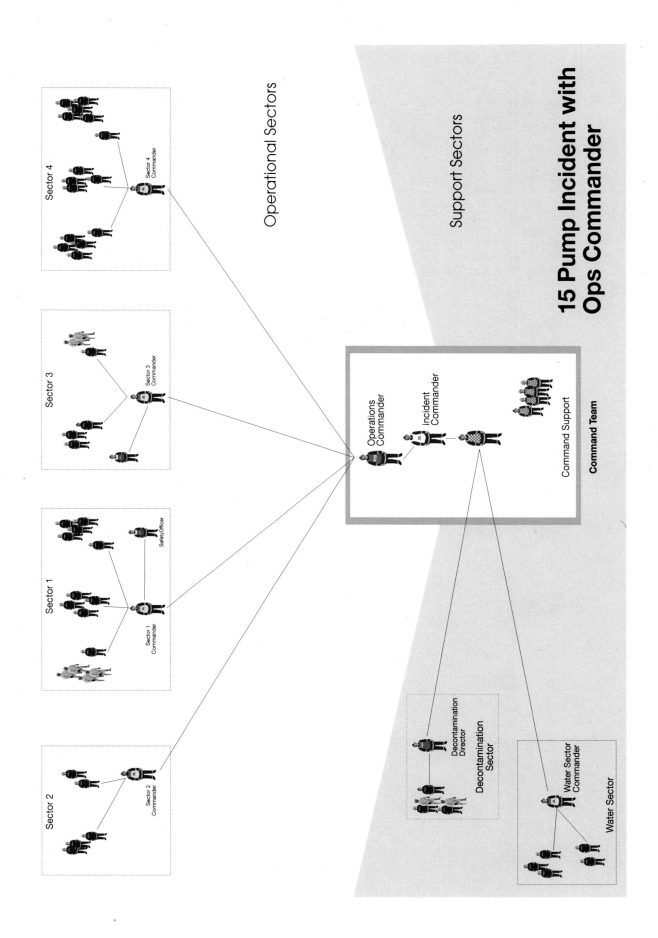

15 Pump Incident with Ops Commander

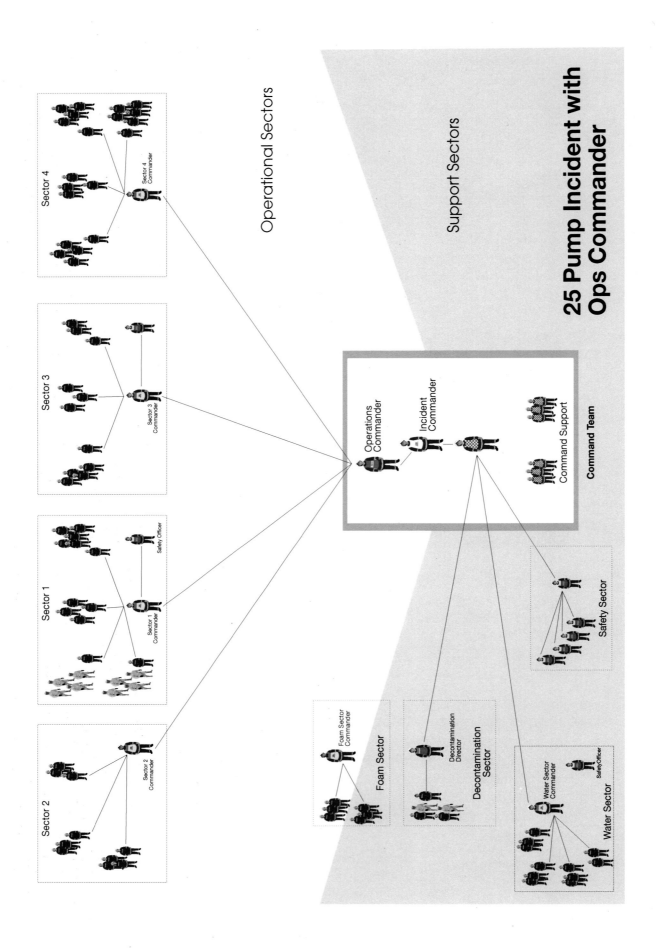

25 Pump Incident with Ops Commander

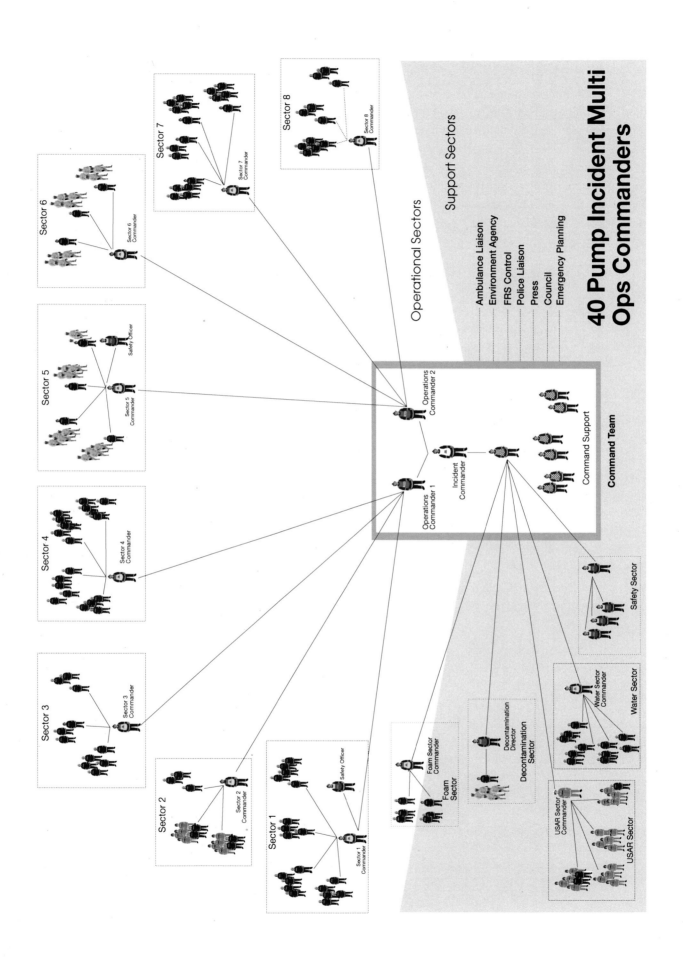

40 Pump Incident Multi
Ops Commanders

Operational Sectors

Support Sectors

Sector 6
Sector 6 Commander

Sector 5
Sector 5 Commander
Safety Officer

Sector 4
Sector 4 Commander

Sector 7
Sector 7 Commander

Sector 8
Sector 8 Commander

Sector 3
Sector 3 Commander

Sector 2
Sector 2 Commander

Sector 1
Sector 1 Commander
Safety Officer

Operations Commander 2

Operations Commander 1

Incident Commander

Command Support

Command Team

Ambulance Liaison
Environment Agency
FRS Control
Police Liaison
Press
Council
Emergency Planning

Foam Sector Commander
Foam Sector

Decontamination Director
Decontamination Sector

Water Sector Commander
Water Sector

Safety Sector

USAR Sector Commander
USAR Sector

2.13 Briefing & Information

Effective communication is of critical importance at all incidents. Information has to be relayed accurately from the IC to the crews carrying out the work and vice-versa so that the crews are aware of the tactics being employed and the IC is aware of developments on the incident ground. The IC also has a duty to relay messages and information back to mobilising control to ensure an accurate picture of the incident is maintained and recorded.

The effective briefing of crews is essential. This may commence en route to an incident and will be supplemented on arrival once a risk assessment has been performed. Following the initial assessment, crews will be briefed as to the tasks to be undertaken and the hazards and risks they will face. The extent of the briefing will depend largely on the nature and extent of the incident; the pre-briefing for small fires that crews regularly deal with is likely to be relatively straightforward. On the other hand, at incidents where crews have little experience and where there is a high risk factor, the briefing will need to be comprehensive. The need to debrief crews that have withdrawn from a working area during the incident should not be overlooked as valuable safety critical information may be sourced at this time.

2.14 Communications

The IC must establish effective arrangements for communications. Information is one of the most important assets on the incident ground; information must be gathered, orders issued and situation reports received. The needs of other agencies must be assessed and provided for. Regular situation reports should be passed to the IC from all sectors via the established communication links.

The IC will need to:

1. Establish communication links with FRS control.
2. Ensure that incident ground radio channels and call signs have been correctly allocated.

3. Establish communications with other agencies. (This may employ communications equipment on agreed channels or simple direct verbal communication.)
4. Establish communications with Sector Commanders for regular reporting between sectors and the IC and between Sector Commanders themselves.
5. Utilise local systems. Some new and complex buildings and structures, particularly those extending underground, have communication systems installed for emergency services' use.

The above duties will invariably be the role of Command Support under the guidance of the IC.

2.15 Inter-Agency Liaison

The IC must establish and maintain effective liaison with all other agencies, as appropriate. This will include tactical liaison with other emergency services to co-ordinate operational activities effectively, and liaison with technical specialists whose specific knowledge may be critical in helping to resolve the incident. There is also a need to maintain effective liaison with the media, if in attendance, in order that appropriate and accurate information is made available. This is best done in conjunction with other emergency services and other agencies that are present to avoid conflicting reports.

Where there has been a work-related death the terms of the Work Related Death Protocol[6] will apply. The police will initially be responsible for investigating the death and may require assistance in securing evidence. The Protocol is between the police, Health and Safety Executive, Crown Prosecution Service and the Local Government Association. The Office of the Rail Regulator, Rail Accident Investigation Branch, Civil Aviation Authority, Maritime and Coastguard Agency and the Fire and Rescue Service have agreed to abide by the principles of the Protocol.

6 *Work-related deaths: a protocol for liaison* available on HSE's website

The command structures and responsibilities of the other emergency services are summarised in Chapter 3. The methods in which services relate to each other is described in the publication 'Emergency Response and Recovery' HM Government November 2005, non statutory guidance to the Civil Contingencies Act 2004 Ch 3 Responding Agencies, 2005.

2.16   Cordon Control

Cordons are employed as an effective method of controlling resources and maintaining safety on the incident ground. The IC must consider the safety of fire-fighters, the public, members of other emergency services and voluntary agencies attending. However, it must be noted that overall responsibility for the health and safety of personnel working within the inner cordon remains with the individual agencies. Such agencies should ensure that personnel arriving at the scene have appropriate PPE and are adequately trained and briefed for the work they are to undertake within the cordon. Where this is not the case, the matter must be referred to the command level.

After the initial cordon has been established to secure the scene, usually by the police, the incident is usually divided into two types of cordon:

2.16.1 Inner Cordon

An inner cordon is used to control access to the immediate scene of operations. Access to the area controlled by an inner cordon, which by definition is a high hazard zone, should be restricted to the minimum numbers required for work to be undertaken safely and effectively. However, if the incident is the consequence of a suspected criminal act, the police will assume overall control of the area and liaison between the two services will determine entry and exit protocol. Personnel should only enter when they have received a full briefing and been allocated specific tasks.

The Civil Contingencies Act guidance document entitled 'Emergency Response and Recovery' states in Section 3.7 that "Fire and Rescue Services are trained and equipped to manage 'gateways' into the inner cordon, if requested to do so by the police". Capacity to discharge this responsibility varies considerably across the UK, therefore it is important that local planning and exercising is conducted to ensure misunderstandings about roles and responsibilities do not occur during an incident.

In terms of accounting for the safety and whereabouts of personnel, it is already a responsibility of ICs, delegated to Sector Commanders when the incident has been sectorised, to be aware of which personnel and crews are active in their sector. This responsibility may be more effectively discharged if the Sector Commander has a sector command folder or board, as used by some FRS's already. The addition of space for other agencies' personnel, together with checklists for PPE, escorts if necessary, and details of working location, is a minor but necessary addition. It would also be necessary to consider a safety briefing, a record of their presence and agreed evacuation signals.

2.16.2 Outer Cordon

This is used to prevent access by the public into an area used by the emergency services while they are attending an incident. The police will usually control outer cordons. A traffic cordon may then further supplement the outer cordon and the police, in liaison with the FRS and the ambulance service, will identify safe routes into and out of the cordon for further emergency vehicles and other attending agencies.

Marshalling areas will usually be located within the outer cordon area if one or more are established.

2.17 The Closing Stage of the Incident

So far only the initial and developing stages of an incident have been addressed, however the closing stages must also be considered and complacency must be avoided. The key activities involved in the closing stages of an incident are:

- Maintaining control and transfer of health and safety
- Welfare

- Post-incident considerations

2.18 Maintaining Control

The process of task and hazard identification, assessment of risk, planning, organisation, control, monitoring and review of the control measures must continue until the last appliance leaves the incident ground.

As the urgency of the situation diminishes, the IC may wish to nominate an officer to gather information for the post-incident review. In some cases this officer should start to take brief statements from crews before they leave the incident, whilst events are still fresh in their minds, these records may form part of the contemporaneous notes should they be required.

Details of all near misses i.e. occurrences that could have caused injury must be recorded because experience has shown that there are many near misses for every accident that causes harm. There is usually no reason for having to accept significant operational risks at this stage. At the closing stages of the incident, the responsibility for health and safety must be handed over to the appropriate person.

At the closing stages of the incident the responsibility for health and safety must be handed over to the appropriate person.

2.19 Welfare

The welfare of personnel is an important consideration. It must be given particular attention by the command team at arduous or protracted incidents where the normal replacement of personnel is delayed or prevented. Supervisors will continually monitor the physical condition of crews, and where necessary relief crews must be anticipated and managed in an appropriate way.

Welfare considerations such as the provision of food and drink, toilet facilities and possibly shelter from the elements should, where possible, be provided outside the immediate incident area and always away from any risk of direct or indirect contamination.

2.20 Debriefing

The IC and anyone nominated to gather information at the incident should supervise completion of any necessary documentation and ensure that this is complete, accurate and able to be made available promptly.

Debriefing plays an important part in promoting improvements in personal and organisational performance and should take place whenever there is an opportunity to improve standards of service delivery. Such post-incident reviews may be informal or formal; they can range from something as simple as brief discussions on return to station from a minor incident, to a large multi-agency debrief or a Public Enquiry following a major incident. The format chosen for the review should be appropriate to the nature of the incident attended and should be conducted in a manner that promotes open, supportive and constructive discussion of all aspects of the incident. If the performance of individuals is considered in the review, then this should be measured against the standards relevant to the role of each individual. Effective performance and meritorious conduct should be acknowledged where appropriate.

Following an incident, any significant information gained or lessons learned relating to existing operational intelligence information must be fed back into the policy and procedures of the organisation. This includes personal protective equipment (PPE), the provision and use of communications, other systems of work, instruction, training, and levels of safety supervision etc.

It is equally important to highlight any unconventional methods or procedures which were used successfully or made the working environment safer.

Where a formal post-incident review is required it should be held at a venue that is suitable and convenient for those to be invited to attend. Copies of relevant documentation should be available and provision made for recording proceedings, outcomes and learning points. Notes of the outcomes and details of action taken, or planned, to address the learning points raised should be made available to the relevant people as soon as practicable.

2.21 Post-Incident Considerations

The majority of the activities and processes centre around the emergency phase of an incident. However, there are issues which involve the FRS for well beyond the emergency phase. Examples include the following:

- Post-mortem enquiries and Coroner's hearings
- Fire investigation
- Accident investigation (where a death has or may result then the 'Work Related Death Protocol' must be adhered)
- Public or judicial enquiries
- Litigation
- Financial costs to the brigade i.e. damaged equipment
- Criminal Investigation
- Incident debriefing and evaluation
- Fire safety issues
- Learning and recommendations, both local and national
- Critical incident – ongoing emotional and welfare support

The IC must, at the earliest convenient time, attempt to assess what the post-incident considerations might be. On the basis of this assessment, the following tasks might need to be undertaken:

1. Scene Preservation: As soon as it is identified that detailed examination of the scene might be required as part of a criminal investigation, efforts must be made to preserve the scene from any further interference and to secure

evidence. Where there is a work-related fatality the procedures in the Work Related Death Protocol should be followed.

2. Recording and Logging: This might include a written log available from FRS control room, in the Command Unit during the incident or voice recording of critical messages. The early attendance and planned deployment of service photographic/video personnel can prove to be of great benefit in this area. The obtaining of security videos from on-site equipment can often be of value in subsequent investigations. Action on this matter needs to be taken without delay, as some systems will re-use the tapes.

3. Impounding Equipment: Where accidents or faults have occurred, any associated equipment should be preserved for later investigation. Should major malfunction of FRS equipment occur, in addition to the normal required notification being carried out, any associated guidance involving any external agency or department (i.e. Health and Safety Executive) which it is a requirement to inform, should be observed.

4. Identification of Key Personnel: The names and location of witnesses to important events should be obtained and recorded for later interviews. It may be necessary or appropriate to commence interviewing during the incident.

5. Managing the closure of the incident: This includes considerations such as proper handovers as the incident reduces in size, continued vigilance regarding the hazards that continue to exist or newly emerge, making appliances and crews available again at the earliest possible time, and ensuring that site occupiers, neighbours and others who have been affected by the incident are kept appropriately informed.

6. Before finally closing an incident and withdrawing all FRS resources, the IC should inform the person having ongoing responsibility for health and safety on the incident ground, or their agents, that FRS operations have closed down and indicate all hazards still present. In the absence of advice from other appropriate agencies, the IC may wish to give advice on how the hazards may ultimately be dealt with and advice about appropriate interim control measures. The IC must ensure that the responsible person fully understands the hazards and accepts responsibility for ensuring health and safety on the site; this may include the control of potential environmental hazards caused by FRS operations.

7. In a similar way, security issues, particularly where premises are left vulnerable, must be properly communicated to those accepting responsibility from the FRS commander. FRS's may wish to consider some form of documentary evidence of this kind of handover.

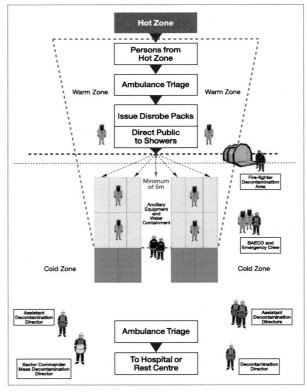

Detail of Mass Decontamination Team structure – see diagram page 49

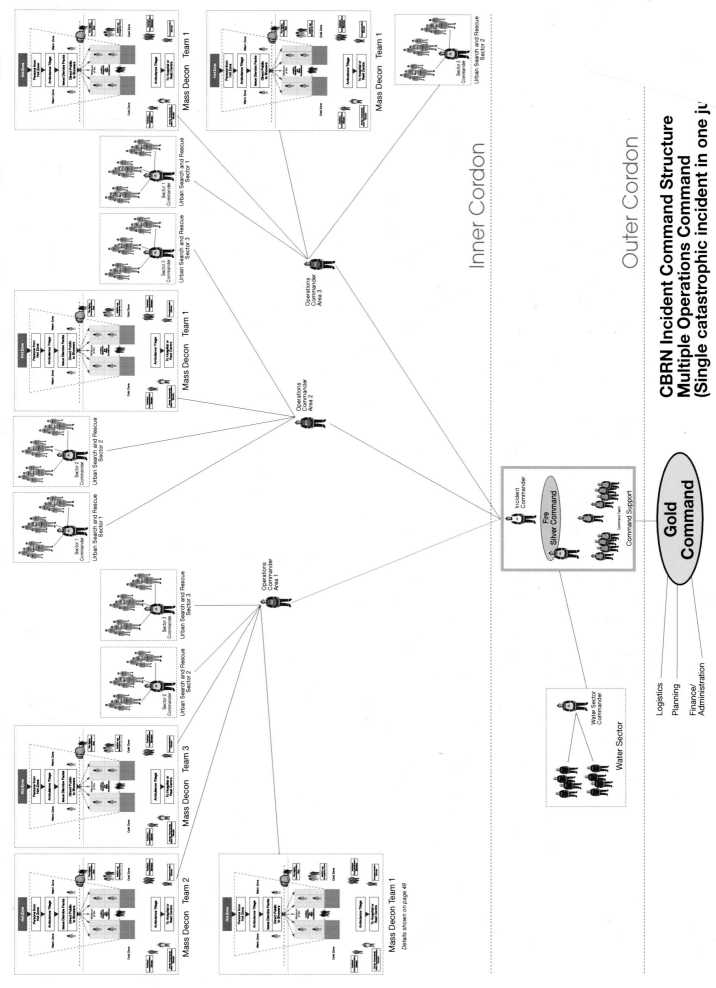

CBRN Incident Command Structure
Multiple Operations Command
(Single catastrophic incident in one ju

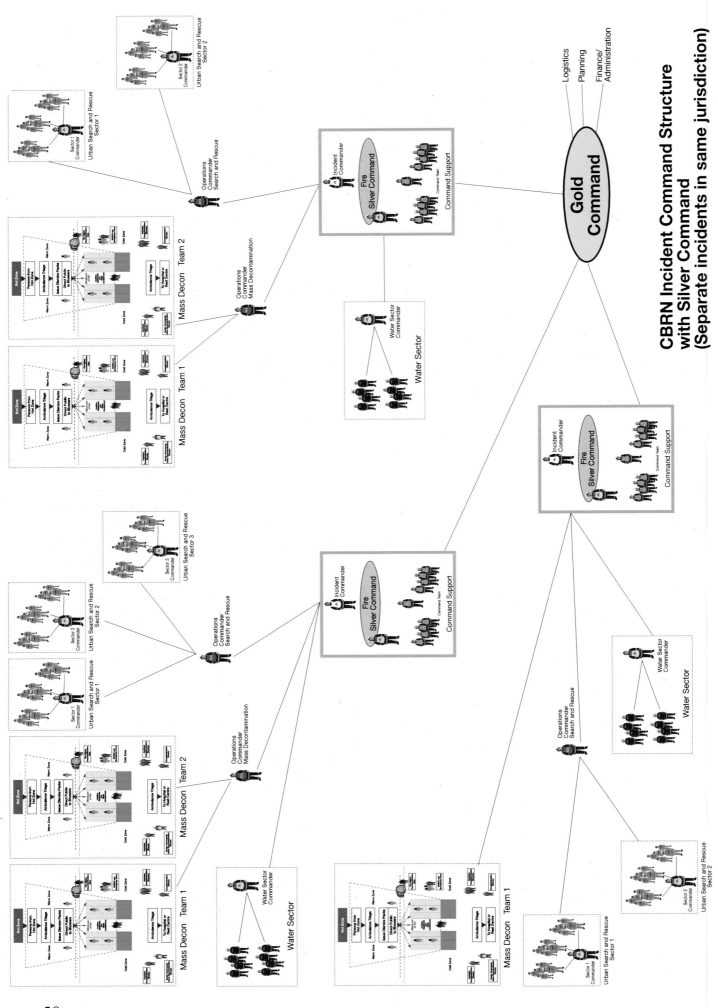

**CBRN Incident Command Structure
with Silver Command
(Separate incidents in same jurisdiction)**

Chapter 3 – Command within the UK Resilience Framework

3.1 Introduction

Management and command of the most serious incidents is rarely a single agency task. The Incident Command system was developed to ensure that FRS structures and protocols would fit seamlessly with those of partner organisations and the UK's overall approach to integrated emergency management. That approach has been significantly revised and updated to reflect the new nature of the risks and threats that the country faces on a daily basis, and is formalised in the Civil Contingencies Act 2004, including associated guidance and regulations. FRS commanders need to understand clearly the various entities, and players, at various levels within the UK's resilience framework, including knowledge of the powers and duties of officials at key levels. This chapter examines that framework.

The Civil Contingencies Act 2004 (CCA 2004) brought together elements of a number of older statutory provisions, including the Defence of the Realm Act of 1914, the Emergency Powers Acts of 1920 and 1964 and the Civil Defence Act 1948, which have all now been repealed (with the exception of S.2 of the Emergency Powers Act of 1964, which allows the Defence Council to authorise "the temporary deployment of Service personnel on urgent work of national importance").

The UK's emergency preparedness was previously closely linked with the civil defence framework that developed post World War Two, during the period of the cold war. Even before that, the focus was clearly changing, with the Civil Protection in Peacetime Act 1986 making provision for resources previously allocated to civil defence to be used in preparation for peacetime emergencies. By the mid 1990's it was clear that the civil defence and emergency planning framework was no longer fit for purpose. A review was commenced involving all the major stakeholders, including local authorities, emergency services, and other government departments. Issues such as the "Y2K Millennium Bug", or millennium date change problem, became typical of the type of issue attracting attention from the planning and response communities, as did the fuel crisis, foot and mouth disease and other non-hostile action types of risk.

This perspective changed on 11th September 2001, or "9/11". The subsequent consultation and preparations, and resulting legislation, primarily the CCA 2004, and for FRSs the Fire and Rescue Services Act of 2004, has provided an expanded range of duties. This has been accompanied by detailed guidance for authorities to ensure that they will be able to deliver what is expected of them at the required times, be able to work effectively with other partners, and have means in place to continue their operations at times of challenge to their own infrastructures.

For FRSs, the post 9/11 environment demanded that their own capabilities be developed to cope with a wider range of disruptive challenges to the community. This programme, which became known as the "New Dimension" programme, delivered the capability to deal with mass decontamination incidents; to detect, identify and monitor chemical substances; pump high volumes of water over large distances; search for, and rescue persons from, urban collapses, landslides etc; and effectively command and control the large scale of operations that may be necessary when bringing these capabilities into play.

The Civil Contingencies Act 2004 Part 1 covers 'arrangements for civil protection'. The Act applies to England, Scotland and Wales with some differences in application. In Scotland, civil protection is a devolved matter and therefore the responsibility of the Scottish Executive, whereas the Welsh Assembly Government in Wales exercises authority. *In Northern Ireland the 'Civil Contingencies framework' discharges the principles contained within the Civil Contingencies Act 2004. (The Fire & Rescue Service is not a Category One Responder in Northern Ireland).* In general Category One and Two Responders are obliged to co-operate with each other and other organisations engaged in response in the same local resilience area. Each local residence area is based on a police area.

A more detailed explanation of the slight differences of the arrangements within the devolved administrations will be found in the Appendices 5 to 7.

Category One and Two Responders have a duty to share information with each other. Information sharing is considered both good practice, and also essential to underpin co-operation. Although there is an initial presumption that all information can be shared, there are in fact certain limits on disclosure. It is important when working in this field to understand the categorisation of information, and the constraints on how it may be used. This is described in Chapter 3 of the document entitled Emergency Preparedness (HM Government, November 2005); statutory guidance that supports the Civil Contingency Act 2004.

3.2   Local and Regional Structures

Before considering the FRS roles and responsibilities, the local and regional structures and machinery that come into play during times of crisis or major emergency should be examined.

3.2.1   Government Offices of the Regions

The nine Regional Government Offices (GOs) offer a single point of access to central government for local responders in English regions. The GOs are likely to have a role in most emergencies that could generate ministerial interest or national/regional press coverage. Government departments may also use GOs to cascade information and guidance to local responders. Regional Resilience Teams (RRT) have been set up in each of the GOs to co-ordinate the response of the whole GO area, and to act as the first point of contact for any resilience issues in normal working hours. RRTs act as support for lead government departments' representatives when they need to operate in the regions or support Gold level or other operational decision making groups during emergencies.

3.2.2   Government Liaison Team

Government Office provides the focus for communication to and from the Strategic Co-ordinating Group (SCG), the Lead Government Department and the Government Liaison Team (GLT). This would be headed by a senior Home Office official in the event of the incident being a result of terrorist action. Otherwise the team would normally be headed by the Regional Resilience Director of the GO. The team consists of representatives from central government who assist the Gold Commander by:

- Keeping the Cabinet Office Briefing Room (COBR) fully informed of the involvement of the incident.
- Accelerating liaison between the Gold Commander and COBR when Central Government involvement is required in decision making.
- Ensuring that the local interest is taken fully into account at COBR, and conversely to ensure that the Government's views are kept in mind at the scene.
- Ensuring smooth communication flow between COBR and the incident.

3.2.3 The Local Resilience Forum

The Local Resilience Forum (LRF), comprising Category 1 Responders as defined by the Civil Contingencies Act 2004, is the basic mechanism through which local government, emergency services and utility services co-operate under the Act. The Act requires that Category 1 Responders attend the LRF, and the guidance offers model terms of reference for it, which includes ensuring joint policy positions, risk assessments, planning, exercising etc.

Category One Responders under the CC Act include:

Local authorities
Police (local and British Transport Police)
Fire and Rescue Authorities
Ambulance Services
National Health Service (including Primary Care Trusts, Strategic Health Authorities and Local Health Boards)
Health Protection Agency (the HPA will represent port health authorities if applicable)
Environment Agency
Maritime and Coastguard Agency

Category Two Responders under the CC Act include:

Electricity distributors and transmitters
Gas distributors
Water and sewerage undertakers
Telephone service providers
Railway operators
Airport operators
Ports
Highways Agency
HSE

Other Co-operating Bodies under the CCA include:

Regional Resilience Teams
Military
Voluntary Sector

It is often the individual officials who represent their organisations as LRF members who find themselves with operational responsibilities during the emergency response phase. Therefore, in effect, the LRF constitutes the group of responders engaged in planning and preparation, which becomes the Strategic Coordinating Group (SCG) or multi-agency Gold group, in times of emergency response.

An LRF may be chaired by a representative of any Category One Responder organisation, but in most cases this function is undertaken by the police. Equally, the secretariat for the group will be provided by one of the leading Category 1 Responder organisations, often a local authority.

The provisions of the Regulations in Scotland are largely the same as in England and Wales, however the LRF is called the Strategic Co-ordinating Group, which if not properly understood gives potential for misunderstanding with the English model. Additional Regulations made by Scottish Ministers determine how Category One and Two Responders within devolved administrations should co-operate with each other.

3.2.4   The Regional Resilience Forum

Unlike LRFs, Regional Resilience Forums (RRF's) are not statutory bodies. They are not hierarchically superior to LRFs or inferior to other national level committees. This status is defined as "subsidiary". An RRF's main function is to provide regional co-ordination of multi-agency resilience activities and delivery. A RRF will undertake a range of functions, including compiling a regional risk map; considering policy initiatives in the area of civil protection that emanate from government; facilitating information sharing, including lessons from exercises and incidents at home and abroad, and co-ordinating multi-agency exercises and training. RRFs are usually chaired by the Regional Resilience Director of the Government Office of the Region. The main exception is that in London this function is performed by the Minister of the Crown with the London portfolio. London is unusual in the fact that the LRF and the RRF are effectively the same body, given the boundaries of the Metropolitan Police Service, which is co-terminous with the area of the London Fire Brigade and the London Ambulance Service.

3.2.5   The Regional Civil Contingencies Committee

In a similar way to an LRF which will, at times of emergency, convene operationally in the guise of a Strategic Co-ordinating Group, the RRF member organisations may convene as a Regional Civil Contingencies Committee (RCCC) On occasions the same individual may represent their organisation in both LRF and RRF arenas. This is usually a consequence of a particular organisation's geographical and operational boundaries.

The RCCC can come into play to co-ordinate the response to, and recovery from, an emergency at regional level in England. The RCCC is likely to be convened only rarely and only when it can add value to a response.

There are three levels of RCCC meetings;

Level 1 – Preparedness in the phase prior to an Emergency

Level 2 – Co-ordination of Response in the Region.

Level 3 – Declaration of Special Legislative Measures.

The role at Level One, where the committee will be chaired by the GO Director, is one of monitoring and assessing the situation which may be developing, and establishing a state of preparedness.

Level Two meetings are intended to co-ordinate a response to an emergency across a region. It is possible that a request to perform this role would come from a Strategic Co-ordinating Group at a local level. Level Two meetings are also co-ordinated by the GO Director, or in the case of an event where a clear lead from a government department could be identified, e.g. a health or veterinary crisis, then the chair would be provided by that department.

Level Three meetings are only called when Emergency Powers under Part Two of the Civil Contingencies Act 2004 have been invoked and have to be managed. A Level Three meeting would be chaired by a Regional Nominated Co-ordinator,

appointed by central government, to deliver the strategic objectives set by government to resolve the emergency.

3.3 Central Government's Role

Although the vast majority of crises, however significant, are handled effectively at local level, from time to time, in the most complex and large scale incidents, central government support and co-ordination is necessary to control the emergency. Government will consider the overall strategic position and provide direction where necessary. Information will be provided from a range of sources, including the local SCGs, the Joint Terrorism Analysis Centre (JTAC), scientific advisory groups via the Lead Government Department (LGD) and other key stakeholders. Consideration may be given to such issues as the mobilisation of national assets and military resources, managing the public information and international or diplomatic aspects of the emergency, ensuring a common picture of the situation is developed, and assessing the likely development of the situation to enable the recovery phase to commence as early as possible. Central government will also make decisions involving the prioritisation of use of scarce resources during multi-site incidents, consulting the devolved administrations where appropriate, and give consideration to whether existing legislation is adequate to cope with the challenge, and if not, implement emergency powers.

3.3.1 Cabinet Office Briefing Room

The Cabinet Office Briefing Room (COBR, sometimes referred to as "Cobra") can be activated to support the co-ordination and decision making that may be required. Officials and key stakeholders will meet and prepare advice for ministers on the most pressing issues.

There are three levels of emergency described in the central government's concept of operations:

Level 1

"Significant": In this case the Lead Government Department (LGD) leads. The COBR facility is not fully activated but provides cross-government co-ordination. Examples of this level would be prison riots or severe weather.

Level 2

"Serious": At this level where the situation threatens a wide or prolonged impact COBR is activated, Cabinet Office or the LGD would chair meetings of officials.

Level 3

"Catastrophic": Where the situation threatens the highest and most serious level of impact COBR would be fully activated and lead the response. It is likely that the Prime Minister or a senior cabinet level minister would chair the meetings.

3.4 Roles of the Emergency Services and Military

Chapter 3 of the document entitled 'Emergency Response and Recovery' HM Government 2005 outlines the roles and responsibilities of each of the main agencies and sectors that are likely to become engaged in the response to, and the recovery from an incident.

3.4.1 Role of the Fire and Rescue Service

The primary role of the FRS in an emergency is to rescue people trapped by fire, wreckage or debris, and to prevent further escalation of an incident by controlling or extinguishing fires and taking other preventative measures. Other responsibilities include:

- Dealing with released chemicals or other contaminants in order to render the incident site safe or recommend exclusion zones.

- Assist other agencies with the removal of large quantities of flood water.
- Assist the Ambulance Service with casualty handling and the police with body recovery.
- Manage gateways into the inner cordon if requested to do so by the police, recording the entry and exit of personnel. Note: the health and safety of personnel working in the inner cordon remains with the individual agencies, however in the absence of appropriate personal protective equipment (PPE), refusal into the risk area should be considered.
- Assist the National Health Service (NHS) with the decontamination of casualties by undertaking where required the mass decontamination of the general public where large numbers of people have been exposed to chemical, biological, radiological or nuclear substances (CBRN).

3.4.2 Role of the Police

The police will co-ordinate the activities of those responding at and around the scene of a land based sudden impact emergency. The saving and protection of life is the priority, but as far as possible the scene is to be preserved to safeguard evidence for subsequent investigations. Other responsibilities include:

Establishing and maintaining cordons around the incident, in particular an outer cordon to facilitate the work of other agencies.

- Where terrorist action is suspected the police will assume overall control of an incident.
- Carrying out a search for secondary devices and performing an assessment of associated risks involving terrorist incidents.
- Oversee any criminal investigation including the preservation and retrieval of evidence.
- Process information surrounding casualties and the identification and removal of fatalities on behalf of the HM Coroner.

- Co-ordinating search activities on land following an event where it is possible that persons may not be located in the immediate vicinity of a disaster scene.

3.4.3 Role of the Health Service

The role of the Ambulance Service is to co-ordinate the on-site National Health Service (NHS) response, and to determine to which hospital casualties are transported, depending on the types of injuries sustained.

The Ambulance Service will also (in conjunction with a Medical Incident Officer):

- Endeavour to sustain life through effective emergency treatment at the scene.
- Determine the priority for release of trapped casualties and decontamination in conjunction with the Fire and Rescue Service.
- Transport the injured in order of priority to receiving hospitals.

3.4.4 Role of the Military

The national structure, organisation, skills, equipment and training of the Armed Forces may be of benefit to the civil authorities in managing the response to and recovery from emergencies. This support is governed by the Military Aid to Civil Authorities (MACA) arrangements. However the Armed Forces maintain no standing forces for MACA tasks, and assistance will be provided on an availability basis only. Therefore it is essential that responding agencies do not base plans upon the assumption of military assistance. The Armed Forces should only be called upon as a last resort and approval is required by the Defence Minister.

In normal circumstances, the 'concept' of the Lead Government Department taking charge of an event is applied, however in the event of a terrorist attack, or when the local responses are overwhelmed Central Government would take charge.

Military Aid to Civil Authorities supports the civil authorities in the fulfilment of civil objectives, principally in peace. MACA is subdivided into 3 categories:

- Military Aid to other Government Departments (MAGD) – is the aid provided by the Armed forces on urgent work of national importance or in maintaining supplies and services essential to life, health and safety of the community.
- Military Aid to the Civil Power (MACP) – the provision of military assistance (armed if appropriate) to the Civil Power in the maintenance of law, order or public safety. The Civil Power is normally construed as the Chief Constable in the relevant area.
- Military Aid to the Civil Community (MACC) – is the provision of unarmed military assistance:
  - To the civil authorities when they have an urgent need for help to prevent or deal with the aftermath of a natural disaster or a major incident.
  - To civil sponsors, either by carrying out special projects of significant social value to the community or by attaching individual volunteers full-time for specific projects.

3.5 Structured Response to a Major Incident

In order to achieve a combined and co-ordinated response to a major incident the capabilities of the FRS must be closely linked with other agencies. A generic command structure has been agreed nationally which can be employed for all significant incidents. Gold, Silver and Bronze are in common use in most responding organisations, referring to levels of command at Strategic, Tactical and Operational respectively For a detailed examination of the roles at each level please see Chapter 1, and for the operational duties at each level, Chapter 2 of this manual.

3.6 FRS Resilience

The Government's national capabilities programme refers to "resilience" as the ability to manage disruptive challenges, for example, responding to terrorist attacks or other events such as widespread flooding within the UK. Part of this resilience programme is to build capacity in the UK's Fire and Rescue Authorities to be able to deal safely and effectively with major incidents on a local, regional or national level.

The UK FRS's structure for responding to major emergencies has been developed, and updated, to complement, and benefit from, the structures described above.

The New Dimension programme, in conjunction with the Fire and Resilience Directorate of the Department for Communities and Local Government ensured that Fire and Rescue Authorities were suitably equipped and trained to deal safely and effectively with major CBRN and conventional terrorist incidents on a national scale. The "enhanced capability" programme saw the allocation of resources to strategically positioned Fire and Rescue Services of Incident Response Units (IRU), Detection, Identification and Monitoring (DIM) teams, Urban Search and Rescue (USAR) teams, Enhanced Command Support (ECS) and High Volume Pumps (HVPs).

These were part of a range of measures taken to improve resilience in the UK which include the following.

3.6.1 FRS National Co-ordination Centre

The New Dimension programme resulted in many specialist units being located in FRSs across the UK. To ensure that all of this equipment and specialised crews can form a coherent and effective response to catastrophic incidents, the Fire and Rescue Service National Co-ordination Centre (FRSNCC) was established to co-ordinate the mobilisation and deployment of New Dimension in collaboration with local or regional control centres. In the longer term the continued delivery

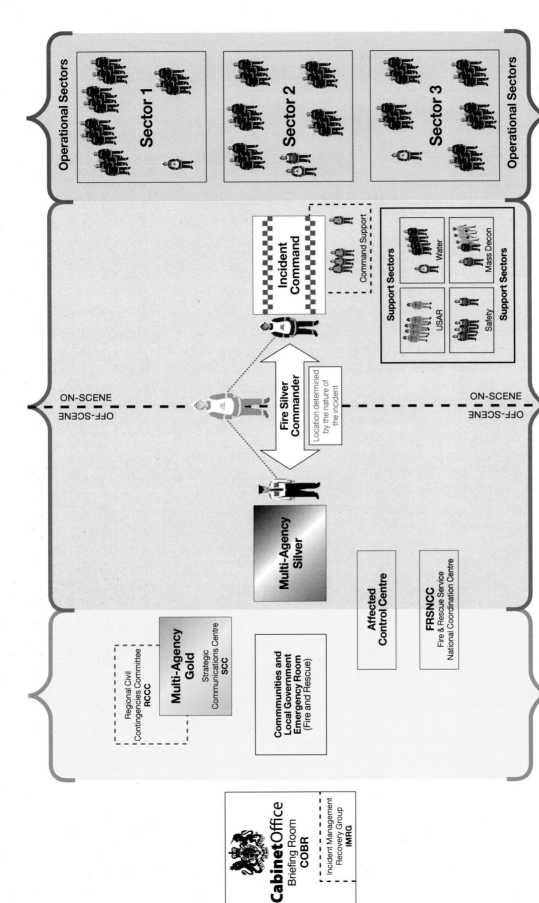

of a robust national co-ordinating capability will be closely linked with the development of Regional Control Centres.

The FRSNCC's principal role is to co-ordinate the national and cross regional mobilisation and deployment of all New Dimension resources in response to a major incident. It will do so in close co-operation with the Communities and Local Government Emergency Room (Fire and Rescue) where these arrangements have been activated, and control room staff in both the affected FRS and those FRSs being asked to assist. To enable it to undertake this role and maintain a database of resource availability, FRSNCC continuously monitors and tracks New Dimension resources, using information provided by Fire and Rescue Services.

3.6.2 FRS Mutual Assistance

The existence of a national mutual aid agreement allows individual Fire and Rescue Authorities to secure assistance from other authorities in the event of a major incident. Authorities have for many years provided mutual support across borders for responses to emergencies through the shared availability of fire crews and appliances. It is important that this good practice is universally applied at local, regional and national level to ensure an effective and efficient response to incidents.

Every FRA in England has agreed to participate under the terms of the National Mutual Aid Programme.[7] Each FRA has confidence in being able to request or provide assistance from each other should a serious incident occur. Full FRA participation in the protocol also means that the task of the FRSNCC co-ordinating New Dimension resources during serious incidents, is greatly assisted. The protocol has enabled FRAs to agree in advance the terms under which they can support each other during an incident such as a terrorist attack.

3.6.3 Convoy Procedure

In planning for large scale incidents, and following the formalisation of national mutual assistance arrangements, it can be seen that from time to time there may be the need to move large numbers of vehicles and personnel around the UK. A guidance note has been issued by the Fire and Resilience Directorate which supports this. All guidance will of course be kept current.

For example, all FRSs have been equipped by Communities and Local Government with the capability to deal with mass decontamination of the public, in the form of Incident Response Units (IRU's). In the event of a Chemical, Biological, Radiological and Nuclear (CBRN) attack anywhere in the UK, the mobilisation of the IRU's and supporting appliances will take place. FRSs are expected to pre-plan for this in conjunction with the guidance document and their respective police force, where Convoy Assembly Points (CAP) will be identified as a starting point.

3.6.4 Strategic Holding Area

Convoys of vehicles converging on a city or other geographical point which has been affected by a serious incident need to be managed and marshalled effectively. Accordingly, Strategic Holding Areas (SHA) have been identified at key locations on the motorway and trunk road network. A SHA is an area which will be used to 'hold' FRS resources and national assets of all kinds in response to an incident. It will be an area with suitable space and facilities to accommodate large numbers of crews, appliances and equipment where these resources can standby, or rest whilst awaiting deployment to marshalling areas and from there to the scenes of operations. The SHAs are part of an overall deployment plan to support the operations on the ground, and of the FRSNCC.

---

7 DCLG 20th July 2006; Fire and Rescue Service Circular 42/2006 invited FRSs to participate in the National Mutual aid Protocol for Serious Incidents; FRSC 75/2006 of 12 Dec 2006 indicated that all FRSs agreed to participate.

The responsibility for co-ordination and communication within the SHA will initially rest with the commander of the Enhanced Command Support facility.

3.6.5 Enhanced Command Support

Enhanced Command Support (ECS) will facilitate the management of national assets following mobilisation to a large incident. It will be adaptable, flexible and complement the ICS.

- It will be located at the SHA and provide a communications link to the IC through Command Support.
- ECS will co-ordinate resources into, within and out of the SHA, facilitating the provision of logistics support to USAR, MD and HVP teams.
- Provide communication links between the IC, FRSNCC, the National Advisory Team members and groups advising senior civil servants and ministers.

- Under the direction of the IC, to facilitate crew reliefs and rotation, and a structured rehabilitation of personnel and equipment to their point of origin in conjunction with the FRSNCC (the FRSNCC will co-ordinate the recovery of ND resources).
- Co-ordinate or conduct additional activities as requested by the FRSNCC or the IC.

3.6.6 FRS National Support Arrangements

At times of the most serious challenge to the Fire and Rescue Services of the UK, and to assist in ensuring that operations are at all times co-ordinated and effective, various teams of advisors have been established to advise government ministers and senior civil servants who may have to make critical decisions that will impact on operations. There will in addition be specialists available to advise Incident Commanders, Sector Commanders and other relevant officials at a tactical and operational level in specialist areas including USAR, MD, HVP, DIM etc.

3.6.7 Communities and Local Government Emergency Room (Fire and Rescue)

During incidents where a FRS has made the request for National support or proactively on receipt of such information which identifies a possible threat to the critical national infrastructure or major emergency , the Communities and Local Government Emergency Room (Fire and Rescue), together with the FRSNCC, will be actively involved in the co-ordination of resources. Certain circumstances could also identify the need for pre-deployment of resources in a preparedness phase to ensure that they are closer to the possible threatened area prior to any occurrence.

During activation the Emergency Room (Fire and Rescue), should be considered as the hub of the advisory and co-ordination framework and will be the key point for providing national advice and co-ordination relating to the use of FRS/Government assets during any major emergency. In close liaison with FRSNCC, personnel will plan and advise on national co-ordination and will be responsible for ensuring that the most effective distribution of FRS/Government assets during any major emergency is achieved with the maintenance of national resilience.

The Emergency Room (Fire and Rescue) will provide comprehensive advice and support capability to the affected FRS, the Fire and Resilience Directorate (FRD) and Ministers, the Cabinet Office Briefing Room (COBR), the Chief Fire and Rescue Adviser (CFRA), the National Strategic Advisor Team (NSAT), and the FRSNCC. Their responsibilities will also include the preparation of timely information in the form of briefings and support to any other key stakeholder as required (e.g. Environmental Agency, PNIC, DEFRA).

The Communities and Local Government Emergency Room (Fire and Rescue) has seven principal roles:

1. Providing structured, trusted advice and secretarial support to Director FRD and the CFRA and event information to other Government departments and Ministers as directed by CFRA or Director of FRD

2. Acting as a FRS central Government hub for the collection, distribution and provision of operational, logistical and policy information relating to FRS activity at events of National significance

3. Linking to the Regional Resilience Teams (the RRT cell offers links through to Government Offices) to provide accurate information on the whole incident to the Director FRD and others as appropriate.

4. Co-ordinating cross Government and international support to assist the Incident Command System

5. Providing cross-government and FRD developed strategic advice to the FRSNCC, Gold Command tier and NSAT

6. Maintaining liaison with FRSNCC and Operational Commanders on the progress of the event(s)

7. To assist with the co-ordination of overseas deployments and reception of teams from outside of the UK (working closely with DFID, EU etc)

Activities in support of these roles could include but not be limited to:

- The proactive cross government/international planning during a major emergency
- Liaison with intelligence services and other relevant bodies
- Assisting with the logistic function responsibility for obtaining additional resources from outside the FRS (e.g. foam from the Ministry of Defence/Civil Aviation Authority/industry or Urban Search and Rescue from the French Government)

- Recognising obstacles that may impact on the affected authority's ability to provide adequate support to the emergency and supporting/prioritising in the areas of concern as quickly as possible to ensure that the response is not adversely affected
- Preparing briefs, guides, submissions to ministers as directed by Director of FRD or the CFRA
- Ensuring that sufficient national cover is being maintained whilst an incident is being managed and prioritising resource deployment in the event that there is more than one incident occurring
- Providing support to the affected FRS as necessary.

- When a decision has been made to seek international support, CLG Emergency Room may have a specific role with arranging this. The UK aims to be self sufficient in dealing with events, and any decision to seek overseas aid would require policy approval, and likely to be brokered through Cabinet office
- Liaison with Devolved Administrations Emergency Rooms.

The Communities and Local Government Emergency Room (Fire and Rescue) main location is London Victoria with a number of contingency fallback locations (Fire Service College and Guildford).

Chapter 4 – Incident Risk Management

4.1 Introduction

The overriding priority of any incident Commander is the safety of all that may be affected by the incident. This must be established by identifying the hazards and risks that are present, identifying and adopting appropriate control measures and ensuring that safe systems of work are implemented and maintained. This will ensure that personnel can carry out their duties and remain safe whilst doing so. Pre-planning is pivotal, where foreseeable events exist generic risk assessments must be carried out. Only after this process can FRS's consider that they have taken all appropriate action to ensure the safety of their personnel and members of the public etc.

The 'Dynamic Management of Risk ' has been defined as: "the continuous process of identifying hazards, assessing risk, taking action to eliminate or reduce risk, monitoring and reviewing, in the rapidly changing circumstances of an operational incident".

There are moral, economic and legal reasons for the FRS to take the 'management of health and safety' seriously.

- **Moral** – As caring employers, organisations want to ensure the safety of their employees at all times.
- As professional bodies, the aim is to discharge their duties to the community to the highest possible standards at all times.
- **Economic** – Good health and safety management is always cost effective. The money invested in safety is always outweighed by the savings in legal costs, compensation, and the need to replace equipment.
- **Legal** – Fire Authorities, in common with other employees have many legal duties in respect of safety. These require employees to ensure, so far as is reasonably practicable, the health, safety and welfare of employees and others affected by their work activities. In order to achieve this they must carry out and record suitable and sufficient risk assessments, then implement the control measures necessary to ensure an acceptable level of safety. Both the risk assessments and the control measures must be regularly monitored and reviewed to confirm their continuing validity.

Employees have a legal duty to take care of their own safety and that of others who may be affected by their acts or omissions. They must also co-operate with their employer in health and safety matters.

To enable an effective risk assessment to be performed it is necessary to understand the following concepts:

- Hazard: which is something with the potential to cause harm, e.g. falling roof tiles
- Risk: which is a measure of the likelihood of harm from a particular hazard occurring and the severity of the consequences, e.g. a fire at derelict property involving the roof may result in an increased risk of injury from falling roof tiles. The severity of this occurrence could be significant if a crew member were hit by the tile.

- Control measure: this is any measure taken to reduce risk, e.g. remove the hazard i.e. roof tiles, or prevent access into the immediate area where harm could be caused. Section 4.11 'Hierarchy of Risk Control' gives further examples of how control measures can be applied at an incident.

In order to provide an acceptable level of protection at operational incidents, the organisations health and safety management must operate at three different levels – Strategic, Systematic and Dynamic.

- Strategic – Strategic health and safety management is carried out by FRS Management Teams and the Fire Authority. They demonstrate management's commitment to safety by setting the organisation's health and safety policy, deciding priorities, providing resources and promoting a positive health and safety culture.

- Systematic – Systematic health and safety management is carried out by recognised departments within the organisation. Initially, risk assessors identify the hazards likely to be encountered at the various types of operational incident and assess the level of risk presented by these hazards. Management Teams act upon the results of the risk assessments and commissions departments to develop and implement additional control measures. These could, for example, be information, personal protective equipment (PPE), and equipment, systems of work, instruction, training and safety supervision.

- Dynamic – Dynamic risk management is carried out by all personnel at an operational incident. The main responsibility lies with the Incident Commander who must identify the hazards, assess the risks, and then make professional judgements in order to use the available resources in such a way as to achieve an acceptable level of safety during work activities.

An important part of risk management at this level is the post incident review. This allows relevant information to be recorded and fed back in to the Strategic decision making process via the Systematic level, in order that safety standards can be constantly improved.

Upon arrival at an incident the first task of the IC must be to gather all available information relating to the incident. This is likely to include information obtained at the pre-planning stage and available on risk cards or electronic storage media. This is in addition to information from the caller, received en-route or passed on by persons already in attendance i.e. occupiers or other agencies.

The IC must then apply professional judgement in conjunction with the Standard Operating Procedures to decide the most appropriate course of action, weighing the benefits of proceeding with a task against the benefits likely to be gained. It is important to 'think before you act rather than act before you think'. The consequences of a wrong decision at this stage may be irreversible.

There will be occasions when rapid intervention may be necessary to effect immediate rescues, or to prevent escalation of the incident. When faced with these situations, personnel are likely to be eager to commence operations immediately on arrival. The highest level of Incident Command will be required to ensure personnel undertaking any role do not act outside agreed safety procedures. In such circumstances, the IC must ensure that personnel are not subjected to unacceptable risks which will outweigh the benefits. It is the responsibility of the IC to carry out a DRA and decide whether operations should continue or adopt a defensive approach until further information has been gathered.

4.2 FRS Operational Risk Philosophy

The benefits of proceeding with a task must be weighed carefully against the risks, it is important to **"think before you act rather than act before you think"**.

The following statements embrace the philosophy of the service's approach to managing risk at an incident:

In a highly calculated way, firefighters:

- **will take some risk to save saveable lives.**
- **may take some risk to save saveable property.**
- **will not take any risk at all to try to save lives or properties that are already lost.**

Therefore, if after implementing all available control measures, the cost (in terms of risk to life) of proceeding with a task still outweighs the benefit, the IC must not permit operations to proceed but consider viable alternative courses of action. This is a critical and defining aspect of operational command responsibility. To discharge this competently requires a detailed knowledge of the principles and regulations surrounding risk assessment and a sound understanding of the factors influencing safety within the 'fire' and rescue domain of the present situation. Pre-

planning should therefore include detailed risk and task analysis and consideration must always be given to ensure that the attendance of critical resources are mobilised as soon as possible.

4.3 Risk Assessment in the Fire Service

Operational procedures and practices are designed to promote safe systems of work. To minimise the risk of injury Incident/Sector Commanders must ensure that recognised safe systems of work are being used so far as is reasonable and practicable. Where possible, operational crews should work together in teams, and whenever practicable the teams should be made up of people who are familiar with each other and have trained together.

When necessary, safety briefings must be carried out and, as the incident develops, or where the risks of injury increases, those briefings must be more precise, and appropriate precautions taken.

4.3.1 Statutory Requirements

Fire and Rescue Authorities, as the employers, have statutory duties towards their employees and others who may be affected by the way in which they carry out their undertaking. Employees also have statutory responsibilities for themselves and anyone who may be affected by their actions or inactions. In practice, high standards of health and safety management can only be achieved if all concerned co-operate in delivering effective and safe systems of work.

Incident Commanders are responsible for implementing safe systems of work at incidents. In deciding whether the health and safety of employees is, so far as is reasonably practicable being ensured, a number of factors have to be taken into account. These include considering the benefit, in terms of saving life, versus risk. Whilst it may be suitable to commit appropriately equipped and trained personnel into a hazardous environment for the purpose of saving life, it may be unsuitable in a similar situation where it is known there are no lives to be saved.

Fire and Rescue Services should carry out suitable and sufficient assessments of the risks involved in responding to incidents. Following paragraphs explain how this requirement is implemented in the FRS, with its wide range of unpredictable and fast-changing incidents. The key elements of the risk assessment process[8] are:

- identification of the hazards;
- decide who might be harmed and how;
- evaluate the risks and decide on precautions;
- record the findings and implement them;
- review the assessment and update if necessary.

The key legal requirements include:

Health and Safety at Work etc. Act 1974

- Section 2 requires employers to ensure, so far as is reasonably practicable, the health, safety and welfare at work of their employees. It also requires employers to have a general policy with respect to the health and safety at work of their employees and the organisation and arrangements for the time being in place for carrying out that policy.
- Section 3 requires employers to conduct their undertaking in such a way as to ensure, so far as is reasonably practicable, that people they do not employ who may be affected are not exposed to risks to their health and safety;
- Section 7 requires employees to take reasonable care of their own health and safety and of the health and safety of others who may be affected by their acts or omissions at work and to co-operate with their employer as far as is necessary to enable the employer to comply with their duties.

Management of Health and Safety at Work Regulations 1999

- Regulation 3 requires employers to make a suitable and sufficient assessment of the risks to the health and safety of their employees to which they are exposed at work and the risks to the health and safety of persons they do not employ arising out of the conduct of their undertaking, to identify the measures that are needed to comply with their statutory duties;
- Regulation 5 requires employers to put in place arrangements for the effective planning, organising, control, monitoring and review of the control measures;
- Regulation 10 requires employers to provide employees with comprehensible and relevant information on the health and safety risks identified by the assessment and the preventive and protective measures;
- Regulation 11 requires employers, where they share a workplace (for example, an incident ground), to co-operate with the other employers and take all reasonable steps to co-ordinate the control measures.

8 INDG163 (rev2) *Five steps to risk assessment* – free on HSE website

4.3.2 Generic Risk Assessment

Due to the scope and nature of FRS operations there are a wide range of activities to cover. This can potentially make risk assessment a time consuming activity. To minimise this and avoid duplication and inconsistent approach, Generic Risk Assessments (GRAs)have been produced to assist FRS with their regulatory requirements. Fire Service Guide, Volume 3 – 'A Guide to Operational Risk Assessment' contains a wide range of risk assessments that all commanders should be aware of when formulating operational plans.

GRAs form the foundation for Dynamic Risk Assessments (DRAs), FRS Standard Operating Procedures (SOPS) and training schemes. They also assist in the completion of Analytical Risk Assessments (ARA's) at incidents (see Appendix 1).

Generic Risk Assessments provide information on

- The scope of the activity
- Significant hazards and risks
- Key control measures
- Technical references
- List of considerations
- Summary (in the form of a table)

4.3.3 Dynamic Risk Assessment

The term Dynamic Risk Assessment (DRA) is used to describe the continuing assessment of risk that is carried out in a rapidly changing environment at incidents (see DRA model in Figure 4.1, p.70). The outcome of a Dynamic Risk Assessment is the declaration of a Tactical Mode (See section 4.5).

Dynamic Risk Assessment takes into account the continually and sometimes rapidly evolving nature of an incident and is a continuous process. This is further complicated for the FRS commander in that often rescues have to be performed, exposures protected and stop jets placed before a complete

appreciation of all material facts has been obtained. It is nevertheless essential that an effective risk assessment is carried out at all operational incidents. In a high risk, low time environment the Incident Commander must implement greater levels of control and apply appropriate control measures, in order to reduce risk to an acceptable level. Only then can crews be committed into the hazard area.

A DRA must be reviewed continuously and updated as required, and as a result of which it is important to declare a 'Tactical Mode'. The mode must be communicated to everyone on the incident ground and transmitted over the main scheme radio where it will be recorded and time stamped. For example, during Offensive operations, new information is received concerning fire spread to a previously unaffected out-building containing cylinders. A new Defensive Tactical Mode should now be declared (See section 4.5.4 Defensive Mode).

Although the dynamic management of risk is continuous throughout the incident, the focus of operational activity will change as the incident evolves. It is useful to consider the process during the three separate stages of an incident

- The Initial Stage
- The Development Stage
- The Closing Stage

4.4 Managing the Risk

If an incident develops to the extent that sectors are designated, Sector Commanders will be responsible for the health and safety of all personnel within their sector. Sector Commanders may feel that they can supervise safety within their own sectors. Alternatively the Sector Commander may feel it necessary to nominate a Safety Officer (see section 4.12). This officer will be responsible to the Sector Commander.

(NB: although the Safety Officer must report to the Incident Commander or Sector Commander, the organisation of the Safety Officers will be managed by the Safety Sector if one has been established.)

As the incident develops, changing circumstances may make the original course of action inappropriate, for example:

- Fire fighting tactics may change from defensive to offensive or vice versa.
- New hazards and their associated risks may arise e.g. the effects of fire on building stability.
- Existing hazards may present different risks.
- Personnel may become fatigued.

Incident and Sector Commanders, therefore, need to manage safety by constantly monitoring the situation and reviewing the effectiveness of existing control measures.

During the development stage of the incident, the DRA will form the basis of the analytical risk assessment (see section 4.10).

4.4.1 Risk Control Process: Initial Stage of Incident

There are 6 steps in the initial assessment of risk:

1. Evaluate the situation
2. Introduce and declare Tactical Mode
3. Select safe systems of work
4. Assess the chosen systems of work
5. Introduce additional control measures
6. Re-assess systems of work and additional control measures

Step 1   Evaluate the situation
The Incident Commander will need to evaluate the situation at the earliest opportunity. This will commence immediately following receipt of the call by reference to information provided during pre-planning arrangements. These take many forms and include 7(2)(d) information, SOP's, fire plans, GRA's etc. On arrival the Incident Commander will need to identify hazards, assess the risk to crews, the public, the environment and analyse resource requirements to decide on the most appropriate course of action.

In order to identify hazards the Incident Commander will initially need to consider:

- Operational intelligence information available from risk cards, fire safety plans, SOPs, GRAs and crews etc.
- Incident information available from the owner or responsible person at the scene.
- The nature of the tasks to be carried out.
- The significant hazards presented by the incident.
- The risks presented to:
  - firefighters,
  - other emergency service personnel,
  - the public and
  - the environment
  - The resources that are available e.g. experienced personnel, appliances and equipment, specialist advice.

Step 2   Introduce and declare Tactical Mode

The declaration of a Tactical Mode, which is the simple expression of whether it is appropriate to proceed to work in a hazard area or not, is a device to enable commanders of dynamic emergency incidents to demonstrate their compliance with the principles of risk assessment and be seen to have done so. The detail of the process can be found in section 4.5. However, in simple terms, after a rapid appraisal of the situation the Incident Commander will either be comfortable in announcing 'offensive mode', which is the most usual mode of operation, or if not must announce 'defensive mode' until sufficient additional information has been gathered, control measures taken, etc. to allow 'offensive' to be declared.

Step 3   Select safe systems of work

The Incident Commander will then need to review the options available in terms of standard procedures. Incident Commanders will need to consider the possible systems of work and choose the most appropriate for the situation.

The starting point for consideration must be procedures that have been agreed in pre-planning and training and those personnel available at the incident have sufficient competence to carry out the tasks safely.

Step 4   Assess the chosen systems of work

Once a course of action, be it offensive or defensive, has been identified Incident Commanders need to make a judgement as to whether or not the risks involved are proportional to the potential benefits of the outcome. If YES proceed with the tasks after ensuring that:

- The objectives, both individual and team are understood.
- Responsibilities have been clearly allocated.
- Safety measures and procedures are understood.

If NO then go back to step 3.

Step 5   Introduce additional control measures

Incident Commanders will need to eliminate, or reduce, any remaining risks to an acceptable level, if possible, by introducing additional control measures, such as use of:

- Personal Protective Equipment e.g. safety glasses, safety harnesses
- Breathing Apparatus
- Specialist personnel or equipment e.g. HP, TL/ALP, USAR
- Safety Officer(s)

Step 6   Re-assess systems of work and additional control measures

The DRA model requires the IC to review the plan based upon changes to existing information and the risks presented to the crews. Once the Tactical Mode has been declared the review process starts. By continually returning to step 1 'evaluate the situation' the cycle continues.

Even when a safe system of work is in place the IC must take into account changing priorities as this may alter the perception of risk. Where risks are present, an assessment of the benefits gained by performing the tasks must be made taking into account the possible consequences. Thus:

- If the benefits outweigh the risks, proceed with the tasks.
- If the risks outweigh the benefit do NOT proceed with the tasks, but consider viable alternatives.

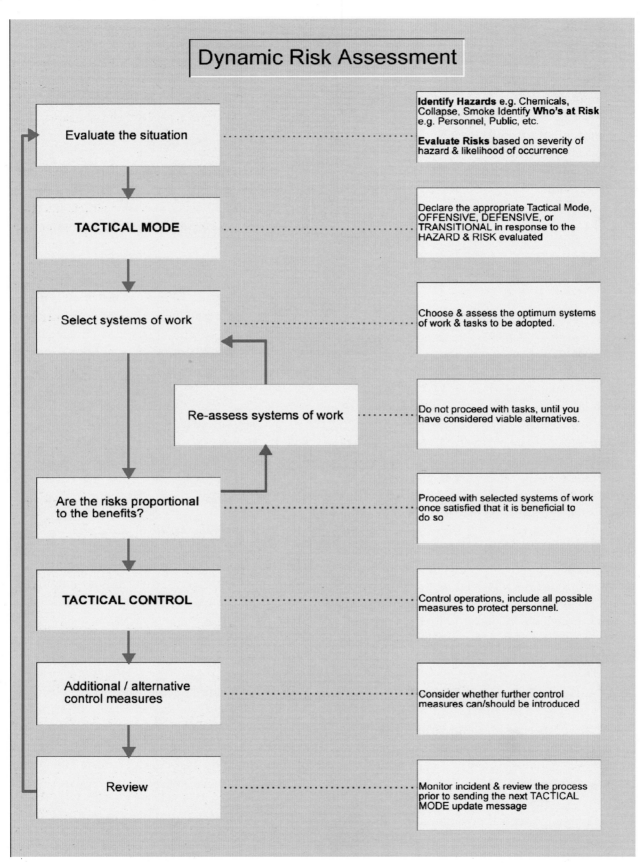

Dynamic Risk Assessment

Evaluate the situation	**Identify Hazards** e.g. Chemicals, Collapse, Smoke Identify **Who's at Risk** e.g. Personnel, Public, etc. **Evaluate Risks** based on severity of hazard & likelihood of occurrence
TACTICAL MODE	Declare the appropriate Tactical Mode, OFFENSIVE, DEFENSIVE, or TRANSITIONAL in response to the HAZARD & RISK evaluated
Select systems of work	Choose & assess the optimum systems of work & tasks to be adopted.
Re-assess systems of work	Do not proceed with tasks, until you have considered viable alternatives.
Are the risks proportional to the benefits?	Proceed with selected systems of work once satisfied that it is beneficial to do so
TACTICAL CONTROL	Control operations, include all possible measures to protect personnel.
Additional / alternative control measures	Consider whether further control measures can/should be introduced
Review	Monitor incident & review the process prior to sending the next TACTICAL MODE update message

Figure 4.1

4.5   The Tactical Mode

4.5.1   General

Tactical Mode is the term used to describe the outcome of the strategic decision which has been taken by the IC which in turn provides the operating framework within which all tactical operations will be conducted. It is often the only strategic decision taken at an incident. A Tactical Mode is required for all incidents and must be kept current at all times.

In any sector or incident which has not been sectorised, there are two possible modes of operation; these are "Offensive" and "Defensive". Where safe systems of work are deployed and adequate control measures implemented the mode of operation is likely to be 'Offensive'. However where the risk to crews is excessive 'Defensive' mode will be declared. Where an incident is sectorised and the mode of operation varies between sectors, i.e. both Offensive and Defensive modes are in operation at the same time at an incident, the incident is deemed to be in "Transitional Mode".

On arrival at an incident the Incident Commander must establish what and where are the most significant hazards to crews. The Incident Commander must be aware that the hazard area may well extend beyond the boundaries of the building. The hazard area is defined as 'an area in which significant hazards have been identified'. The Incident Commander must decide if the level of risk to crews is justifiable within this area'.

4.5.2   Default to Defensive

At a critical incident where immediate action is required, the Incident Commander will make judgement based on the information available, about whether it is safe to proceed with offensive operations. If the Incident Commander determines that the available control measures are insufficient to effectively manage health and safety, a defensive approach must be adopted until a safer alternative approach to dealing with the incident can be implemented.

If the Incident Commander is unsure whether it is safe to announce "Offensive", or confirm offensive operations, then 'Defensive Mode' must be announced. As soon as the Incident Commander is able, a review of the DRA should be conducted. This approach is referred to as 'Default to Defensive'.

The key to effective use of Tactical Mode procedure is speed of application. The process is founded on the psychology of naturalistic decision making and specifically 'recognition primed decision making'. The ability of the Incident Commander to accept risk exposure will be dependent upon the recognition of the adverse impact from an event e.g. the decision versus the risk, this is termed as 'risk appetite'. More details about these theories can be found in Appendix 3 but in application the principles are the same.

Tactical Modes that can be declared at an incident are:

4.5.3   Offensive Mode

This mode may apply to a sector, and/or the entire incident.

This is where the operation is being tackled from within the perceived hazard area. The Incident Commander will have established that potential benefits outweigh the identified risks, so the Incident Commander will be committing crews into a relatively hazardous area, supported by appropriate equipment, procedures and training. Greater levels of control and additional control measures may be required.

Offensive Mode is the normal mode of operation used at, for example, house fires, road traffic collisions and industrial premises to fight the fire, effect rescues or close down plant, etc.

For example, a fire in a derelict property may well be fought from the outside using a jet through a window. This may be a defensive tactic; however operations are carried out within the hazard area (due to the significant hazard of unsecured roof tiles being identified). Offensive Mode would be declared and suitable and sufficient control measures put in place to deal with the risk of falling roof tiles i.e. PPE, crew briefing and safety officers.

Further examples:

- Committing BA crews to a smoke filled or toxic atmosphere (hazard area) to rescue persons or undertake firefighting action is an offensive action.
- Committing crews to a structural collapse (hazard area) to undertake rescues is an offensive action.
- Committing crews into a hazard area at an RTC to perform a rescue is an offensive action.
- Committing a crew to fight a fire in a field is an offensive action.

4.5.4 Defensive Mode

This mode may apply to a sector and/or the entire incident.

This is where the operation is being fought with a defensive position. In Defensive Mode, the identified risks outweighs the potential benefits, so no matter how many additional control measures are put into place the risks are too great.

In these circumstances the Incident Commander would announce Defensive Mode. For example, fight the fire with ground monitor jets and aerial jets and protect exposure risks and adjoining property without committing crews into the hazard area.

Examples of Defensive:

- Withdrawing a crew from a hazardous area because the risk has increased.
- Using jets from outside a hazard area.
- Standing by awaiting expert advice, before committing crews.
- Standing by awaiting specialist equipment.

- Road Traffic Collision involving a chemical tanker leaking a hazardous substance, no persons reported. Crews are standing by awaiting attendance of a specialist advisor and second tanker for decanting.

4.5.5 Transitional Mode

Transitional is declared when both Offensive and Defensive tactics are being carried out at an incident at the same time but in different sectors. It never applies to an individual sector or scene of operation but always to the whole incident.

'Transitional' Mode is not in itself strictly a tactical mode of operation but is a codified description of the incident status signifying that Offensive and Defensive operations are in use in one or more sectors. It is intended to warn personnel that their actions may affect the safety of teams working in a different Tactical Mode in other sectors. For example, crews may be working in 'defensive mode' and using a water tower to fight a fire in a warehouse, however crews from a different sector may have been committed into the building to perform a specific task. By communicating to all personnel throughout the incident ground that the incident is Transitional, this will prompt the Sector Commander responsible for the water tower to consider whether this action may compromise the safety of those inside the building.

4.6 Announcement and Recording of Tactical Mode

A Tactical Mode should be decided upon and announced at all incidents. As the incident grows and the Incident Commander's span of control increases, it is essential that all personnel are aware of the tactics on the incident ground and the prevailing Tactical Mode.

The first first and subsequent informative messages to FRS control should include a confirmation of the Tactical Mode for the information of oncoming appliances and officers. For better clarity over the radio, some FRSs have found it helpful to use the phonetic alphabet to prefix or suffix defensive with 'Delta', offensive with 'Oscar' or transitional with 'Tango'.

A typical Informative Message might be 'Informative message from SM Black at Green Street, Anytown: factory premises, used for textile manufacturing, three floors, 20m x 20m. All floors well alight, three ground monitors in use, "WE ARE IN DEFENSIVE 'DELTA' MODE".

This should then be updated by informing FRS control of which mode the incident is in at frequent intervals or as and when the risk to crews changes (see section 4.10 – Analytical Risk Assessment).

Informing FRS control ensures the recording and time stamping of the decision. When an Analytical Risk Assessment is conducted the outcome is recorded on the appropriate forms.

4.7 Using Tactical Mode when Sectors are in Use

When the incident has been sectorised, the Incident Commander will remain accountable for the Tactical Mode at all times and Sector Commanders are obliged to seek approval for any change of Tactical Mode in their sector. For example, should a Sector Commander wish to deploy personnel into the hazard area, moving from a defensive to an offensive mode, then permission must be sought from the IC. This process is essential for the IC's overall situational awareness of the incident.

However, in an emergency situation the Sector Commander will need to quickly respond to changing conditions e.g. signs of collapse, discovery of cylinders etc. and move from offensive to defensive mode. In such circumstances, the Sector Commander will carry out a DRA, initiate the relevant actions, remove personnel from the hazard area and then inform the IC. Only in exceptional circumstances, such as persons reported, crews in distress etc. may a Sector Commander move from defensive to offensive mode and subsequently advise the IC. The IC will amend the Tactical Mode accordingly in that sector.

Sector Commanders must be involved in any intervention by the IC to amend the Tactical Mode. The change can be implemented effectively and personnel made aware of the current mode in use. However, the proposal to change mode will normally be initiated by the Sector Commander.

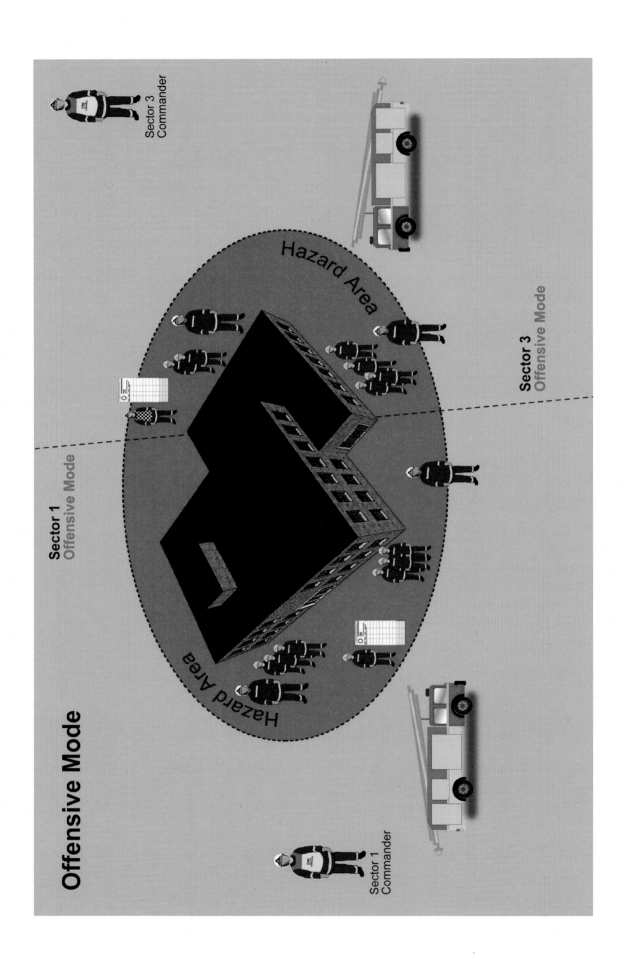

Offensive Mode

Sector 3
Commander

Hazard Area

Sector 3
Offensive Mode

Sector 1
Offensive Mode

Hazard Area

Sector 1
Commander

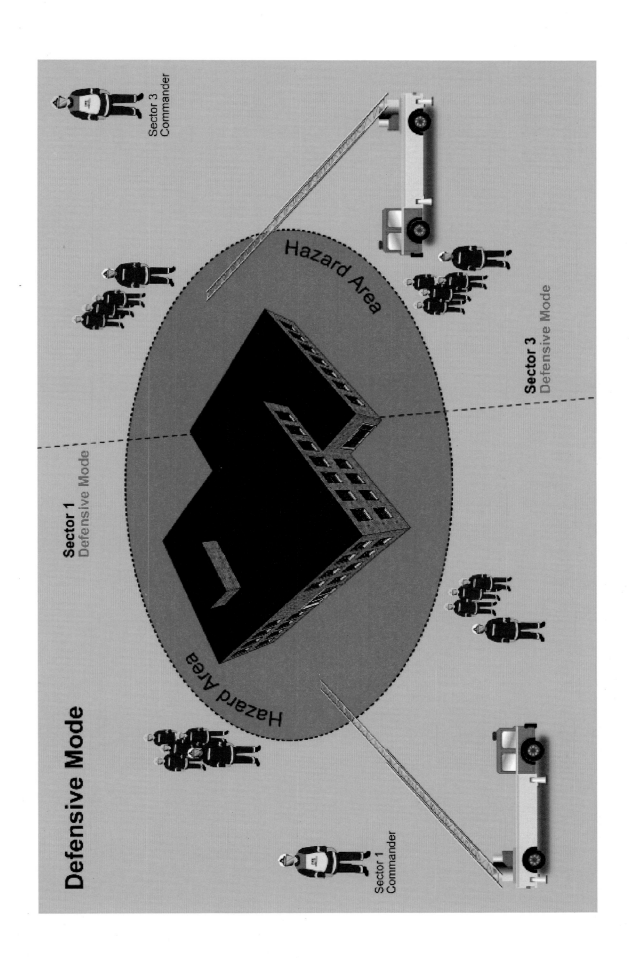

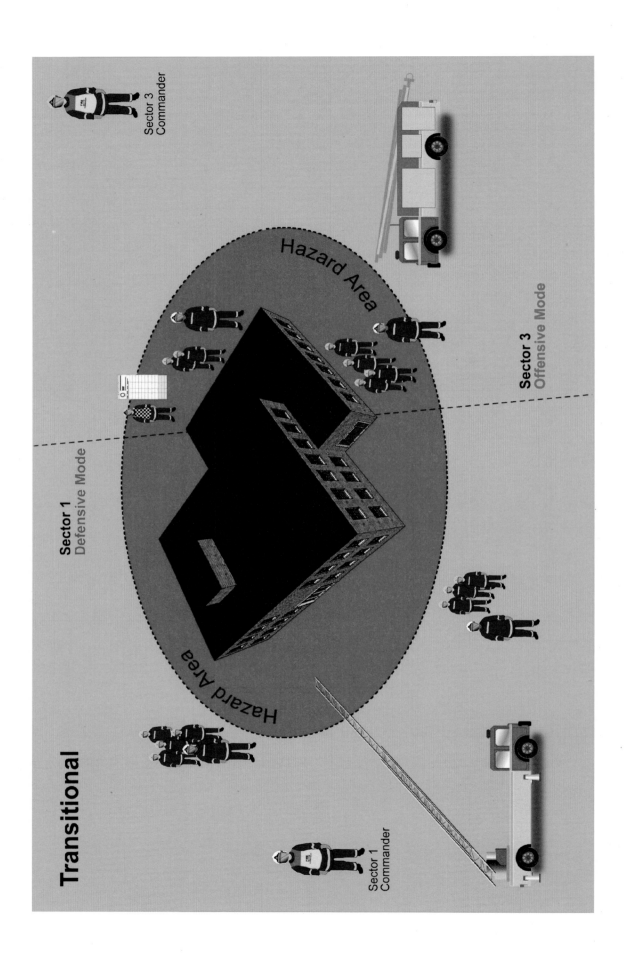

Transitional

Sector 1
Defensive Mode

Sector 3
Offensive Mode

Hazard Area

Hazard Area

Sector 3
Commander

Sector 1
Commander

4.8 Responsibilities within Tactical Mode

Everyone on the incident ground has a responsibility for their safety and the safety of others. Although specific responsibilities are outlined below, if anyone sees anything developing which may compromise the safety of others, they have a clear duty to intervene to prevent harm. This duty is absolute.

4.8.1 Incident Commander

The Incident Commander is at all times accountable for approving and declaring the Tactical Mode. An assessment of the incident should be made and an appropriate plan implemented. The prevailing Tactical Mode should reflect the Incident Commanders plan and associated risks at the incident.

Any message sent should include the current Tactical Mode which is in operation at the incident. This should be repeated at regular intervals or as the risk to crews change, until all FRS operations have finished.

The Incident Commander should review and confirm the Tactical Mode on initial and all subsequent briefings to Crew and Sector Commanders. If appropriate a Safety Officer(s) should be appointed.

Where an Operational Commander has been appointed, they will be responsible for approving changes of the Tactical Mode for the sectors under their control and ensuring that the IC is aware of the prevailing modes at all times.

4.8.2 Sector Commanders

Sector Commanders should continually monitor conditions and operational priorities in the sector and ensure that the prevailing Tactical Mode remains valid. The Sector Commander must liaise with the Incident Commander to ensure the current Tactical Mode is appropriate.

Sector Commanders must immediately react to adverse changes, withdrawing personnel from risk areas without delay if necessary and advise the Incident Commander of the change in conditions as soon as possible thereafter.

If appropriate, Sector Commanders should consider appointing Safety Officers, either for specific areas of concern (e.g. structure stability, dangerous terrain, etc) or for general support. Such Safety Officers should report directly to the Sector Commander but must liaise with other Safety Officers at every opportunity.

It is essential to update the Tactical Mode to the crews working in the sector at a suitably frequent interval.

4.8.3 Crew Commanders

All Crew Commanders should continually monitor conditions in the risk area and draw the attention of the Sector Commander to significant developments, also react immediately to adverse changes and withdraw crew members from the risk area without delay where necessary.

Note: firefighters should also continually monitor conditions in the risk area as part of the Safe Person Concept.

4.9 Examples of Application of Tactical Mode

Example 1
The incident is a 3-pump house fire. The ground floor is well alight and there are persons reported, believed to be in a first floor bedroom. A large jet has been got to work through a front window to knock down the fire on the ground floor.

Two BA teams have been committed from the rear door up the stairs to search the first floor. The incident is not sectorised.

Although a hazard area has been identified by the IC, a decision has been made that crews should operate within that hazard area, so the incident is in Offensive Mode.

Later, the fire on the ground floor has been knocked down. The BA team with a hose reel enters ground floor to continue fire fighting. The incident is still in Offensive Mode.

Example 2
The incident is a 2-pump RTC with persons trapped. Crews are working on the vehicles to carry out rescues. The incident is not sectorised.

Because the vehicle being worked on and the surrounding environment of the roadway etc constitute a hazard area in the opinion of the IC, and a decision has been made that crews should operate within that hazard area, the incident is in Offensive Mode.

Example 3
A 2-pump grass fire occurs on a railway embankment. All firefighting operations are being conducted at a safe distance from either the track or associated overhead line equipment. Crews are standing by awaiting a confirmation that the status of caution has been passed to the rail operator. No personnel have been committed to the embankment and no other operations are under way. The incident is not sectorised.

The IC has identified the main hazard area as the rail track, any overhead line equipment and determined that crews should not venture anywhere near this hazard, therefore the IC declares that the incident is in Defensive Mode.

Later, caution has been confirmed and safe systems of work are being observed. Crews are now working on the embankment but the hazard is much reduced by the control measures which have been taken, so the IC now declares that the incident is in Offensive Mode.

Example 4

A 2-pump RTC with a chemical tanker involved. The tanker is leaking an unidentified substance. No persons are reported trapped. The road is closed and crews are standing by upwind and uphill awaiting attendance of a specialist advisor and second tanker for decanting.

The IC has identified a hazard zone and decided that because neither persons nor the environment is at risk crews will not be committed until the nature of the chemical is established, and specialist advice on tactics obtained. Therefore the IC declares that the incident is in Defensive Mode.

Later, when full hazard information has been received and advice from the Environment agency about potential harm to the environment considered, the IC commits a crew in chemical protection suits to prevent the substance entering a drain. No operations are yet being conducted at the crash scene.

Because crews are now, with suitable protection and using safe systems of work, operating within the hazard zone, the incident is in Offensive Mode.

Example 5

The incident involves a 5-pump retail unit fire in a covered shopping mall. The retail unit is heavily involved in fire, all persons are accounted for. Smoke is issuing from the front of the unit into the shopping mall but is being contained and vented from a large atrium roof space. The smoke level is several metres above the mall floor and is stable.

Operations in the mall are taking place in fresh air and crews are within easy reach of final exits. The back of the unit is outside the mall. Smoke is issuing from the unit's roof and from an open loading bay.

Crews are at work inside the mall with jets into the front of the retail unit. Crews are at work at the rear of the unit with jets through the loading bay. No crews have made an entry to the retail unit.

As a general guide in these circumstances, if conditions within a large building allow a Sector or Incident Commander and associated staff to work within the building, then the risk assessments should be made on the basis of specific areas or compartments within the building rather than the whole building. Commanders and support staff should always work from an area of relative safety, so only crews committed beyond that area into a more hazardous environment could be considered as being committed offensively

Therefore, although crews are inside the mall, the IC has determined that the hazard zone is the affected unit. Because crews are operating outside of the main hazard zone, the IC has declared that the incident is in Defensive Mode.

Example 6

A fire is being dealt with in a multi-occupancy, single story range of premises. Crews in sector 1 are fighting a severe fire in a storage unit with two large jets and an aerial monitor. They are outside the risk area identified by the Sector Commander, therefore they are in defensive mode. Crews in sector 2 and 4 (sector 3 is not in use) are conducting damage control operations in adjoining retail units using BA. They are within an identified risk area, albeit a low risk and are therefore in offensive mode.

Because the incident has been sectorised and 'offensive' and 'defensive' modes are in use, the overall incident is declared as being 'transitional'.

4.10 Analytical Risk Assessment

Having carried out the DRA and established a Tactical Mode, the Incident Commander will be aware of the immediate hazards, the people at risk and the control measures necessary to protect those people. This initial assessment now forms the basis of a more detailed risk assessment, which in the FRS is termed "Analytical Risk Assessment" (ARA).

Due to the continually changing nature of the environment at an incident, the Incident Commander must ensure that as soon as resources permit, an ARA is carried out and, when necessary, new control measures implemented whenever the hazard or degree of risk demands it. The ARA must be recorded. The outcome of the review of the risk assessment will either confirm that the DRA and chosen Tactical Mode was correct, or will result in a change of mode with the appropriate announcements and action occurring without delay. It will also form the basis of a future or ongoing DRA.

At smaller incidents that do not require sectorisation, responsibility for the completion of the analytical review of the risk assessment lies with the Incident Commander or nominated suitable person. At incidents that have been sectorised, the responsibility for the analytical risk assessment may be delegated to the Sector Commanders. The Incident Commander remains accountable for approving the Tactical Mode on all occasions.

The ARA should be kept constantly under review. Whenever the risk to crews changes (or at 20 minute intervals, whichever is the sooner) the Tactical Mode should be reviewed and the risk assessment confirmed or changed as required. Any documentation used should be updated if the information or overall assessment has changed after such a review.

For incidents where a formal debrief may take place, the ARA documentation should be submitted to the Incident Commander for use at the debrief. Analytical Risk Assessments should be kept for audit and periodic review purposes. An example of a procedure to conduct a review and record the outcome of the risk assessment is shown in Appendix 1.

4.11 Risk Control Measures

It has already been discussed that the IC has a decision to make at every incident to determine whether the potential benefits outweighs the identified risks. Where this is the case, the Incident Commander is likely to declare the incident 'Offensive' and commit crews into a 'Hazard Area' to perform an identified role. Where this approach is appropriate the Incident Commander must endeavour to reduce the risks to an acceptable level to complement the training, safe systems of work and specialist equipment the UKFRS has adopted.

The expression 'Hierarchy of Control Measures' is used to detail, in preferential order, measures that may be implemented to eliminate or reduce risk. The mnemonic 'ERIC PD' can be used as a prompt to assist in the process.

- **Eliminate** the risk or substitute it for something less dangerous, e.g. declare defensive mode at an incident thus preventing personnel access into the hazard area, or substitute a hand operated branch for a ground monitor, again removing personnel from the hazard area.
- **Reduce** the risk by preventing or reducing the number of personnel that come into contact with it or reducing the time of the exposure to the risk.
- **Isolate** the risk by separating persons from the risk, e.g. the use of a physical barrier to protect a casualty from cutting operations during extrication from a vehicle following a collision.
- **Control** the risk, e.g. the IC would adopt safe systems of work e.g. tactical ventilation could be used to improve conditions within the building, in conjunction with the appropriate standard operating procedures.
- **Personal** Protective Equipment (PPE), is always the last line of defence because it doesn't contribute to a safer environment, in the FRS it must be assumed that all personnel are provided with suitable and well maintained PPE and that this is utilised at every incident. The use of additional PPE can be requested where circumstance dictates e.g. the use of eye protection at a Road Traffic Collision (RTC) or chemical protection suits at a chemical spill.

- **Discipline** – ensure that discipline is maintained throughout the exposure to the risk; it may be tempting for example to remove PPE while communicating with a casualty at an RTC, where this is in the hazard area personal safety will be compromised. Training plays a key part in maintaining discipline on the incident ground.

It is not possible to implement suitable control measures for an incident prior to arrival and before the subsequent risk assessment is performed. Generic Risk Assessments identify possible hazards, risks and control measures at a range of incidents, thus ensuring personnel adopt a consistent approach to managing risk.

Incident Commanders ideally have access to the appropriate Generic Risk Assessment information whilst en-route or in attendance at an incident, to assist with the identification of suitable control measures. This, in conjunction with other specific facts regarding the premises, for example information gained on risk visits, will assist the IC to formulate an effective plan.

4.12 The Role of a Safety Officer

A Safety Officer may be designated at any time during an incident by either the Incident Commander or Sector Commander as appropriate. This person should be suitably qualified and of appropriate experience. Where appropriate (for example at larger incidents requiring sectorisation) a Safety Officer for the incident may be appointed by the Incident Commander to co-ordinate the role of other Safety Officers and take responsibility for any Health & Safety reporting issues (e.g. accident investigations). In addition, the Safety Officer for the incident, who is referred to as the "Safety Sector Commander" may be responsible for the following:

- To survey operational sectors, identifying hazards, and advise the Sector Commander as appropriate
- To liaise with Sector Safety Officers, to support and exchange information
- To confirm the validity of the initial risk assessment and record as appropriate
- To collate and record Analytical Risk Assessment

- To act as an extra set of eyes and ears to the Sector Commanders in monitoring the safety of personnel
- Liaise with IC or Operations Commander

Safety Officers will be responsible for following list, which is not exhaustive and updating the Incident Commander of any changing circumstances.

- Identify safety issues
- Initiate corrective action
- Maintain safe systems of work;
- Ensure all personnel are wearing appropriate personal protection equipment
- Observe the environment
- Monitor physical condition of personnel
- Regularly review
- Record an Analytical Risk Assessment

The following two examples identify some safety considerations for a safety officer at operational incidents.

Example 1   Derelict property fire

At a fire in a derelict property some of the hazards present may include:

- structural collapse
- difficult access /egress
- unsafe floors and staircases
- the presence of asbestos
- discarded or deliberately placed hypodermic needles or other booby traps
- the unstable state of utilities and services due to vandalism
- poor state of repair of the structure, e.g. roof tiles
- contents and fire loading of building

The likelihood of injury to crews is increased due to state of the building and subsequent hazards. Therefore, it will be necessary to assess the risk to crews against the benefits of saving the building or life should 'persons' be involved.

Possible control measures may include: (this list is not exhaustive)

- evaluate the situation gathering all available information
- declare a Tactical Mode. (As an outcome of the DRA. 'Defensive Mode' would ensure that crews are operating in a safe environment thus reducing risk of injury. Operating in an 'Offensive Mode' would require additional control measures.)
- brief the crews ensuring that all relevant information is passed regarding the hazards, incident objectives and the plan
- committing BA crews in accordance with approved guidance
- ensure a safety jet is provided for the protection of crews
- options for tactical ventilation to reduce or remove smoke and hot gases
- alternative safe means of access and egress
- thermal image cameras for BA crews
- appointing a Safety Officer where resources allow

Example 2   RTC

At a Road Traffic Collision some of the potential hazards may include:

- moving traffic
- vehicles involved and their loads
- airbags, pre-tensioners or hazardous materials
- the occupants of the vehicles or others involved
- broken glass or sharp metal and plastics
- hypodermic needles
- soft and uneven ground where a vehicle has left the carriageway
- contamination by body fluids
- manual handling
- specialist rescue equipment i.e. those operated by hydraulic fluid etc.
- alternative powered vehicles e.g. dual fuel
- fluoroelastomers, fuel/brake fluid lines
- composite materials e.g. carbon fibres

The likelihood of injury to crews is increased due to working in close proximity to the vehicle and subsequent hazards. Therefore, it will be necessary to assess the risk to crews and implement appropriate control measures.

Possible control measures may include: (this list is not exhaustive)

- evaluate the situation gathering all available information
- declare a Tactical Mode as an outcome of the DRA.
- brief the crews ensuring that all relevant information is passed on
- request assistance from the Police for traffic management
- cone area off in the absence of the Police
- wear high visibility clothing
- additional PPE i.e. surgical gloves, eye and ear protection, dust masks etc.
- cover exposed sharp material
- ensure close supervision to ensure correct techniques are adopted
- appointment of a Safety Officer(s)

4.13 Closing Stages of the Incident

During the closing stage of an incident, personnel must not become complacent. The process of task and hazard identification, assessment of risk, planning, organisation, control, monitoring and review of the preventive and protective measures must continue until the last appliance leaves the incident ground.

There are usually fewer reasons for accepting risks at this stage because there are fewer benefits to be gained from the tasks being carried out. Officers should, therefore, have no hesitation in halting work in order to maintain safety.

Debriefing forms an essential part of the management of health and safety on the incident ground. Debriefs may vary in style and content depending upon the scale of the incident. To assist the Incident Commander, an officer can be nominated to help gather information for the debrief. Debriefing will identify any significant information or lessons learnt. Whenever possible, the Incident Commander should debrief crews prior to leaving the incident.

Details of all 'near misses', i.e. events that could have, but did not on this occasion

result in personal injury or equipment damage, must be recorded. Experience has shown that there are a number of near misses prior to an accident occurring. If we fail to eradicate the causes of a near miss, we will probably fail to prevent injury or damage in the future. Appropriate information must then be fed back into the strategic decision making process via the Systematic Level (see reference to HSG 65 below) in order to:

- Review performance of the organisation, team and individuals
- Improve procedures and equipment
- Develop staff and training strategies
- For audit purposes

Equipment, PPE, systems of work and training etc can all be improved as part of this performance management system. HSG 65 – *Successful Health and Safety Management* gives further guidance on the principles of effective health and safety management in the workplace.

It is important to highlight any unconventional system or procedure used which was successful or made the working environment safe. It is equally important to highlight all equipment, systems or procedures which did not work satisfactorily or made the working environment unsafe. More information on closing down incidents and debriefing can be found in Chapter 2 (2.17 and 2.20)

4.14   Summary

- Evaluate situation
- Carry out DRA and announce Tactical Mode
- Communicate Tactical Mode
- Commence operations
- Review Tactical Mode
- A risk assessment must be performed **at all incidents**
- The Incident Commander remains accountable for declaring the Tactical Mode on all occasions
- The Incident Commander may delegate the completion of the Analytical Risk Assessment to other suitable personnel when appropriate
- There are two operational Tactical Modes – **Offensive** and **Defensive**
- Sectors can only be in **Offensive Mode** or **Defensive Mode**
- If combinations of **Offensive Mode** and **Defensive Mode** are in use, the whole incident (which must have been sectorised) will be deemed to be in **Transitional Mode**. This is an operational code which signals to any individual with a responsibility for their own, or others' safety that both offensive and defensive operations are being carried out at the same time.

The Tactical Mode must be current and recorded as appropriate, throughout the incident.

When a Tactical Mode has been decided, the Incident Commander must ensure that everyone on the incident ground is aware of it.

Confirmation of the prevailing Tactical Mode must be maintained between Incident, Sector and Crew Commanders throughout the incident.

Chapter 5 – Command Competence

5.1   Introduction

This chapter explains the term competence and the assessment of competence of the Incident Commander (IC) against National Occupational Standards (NOS).

Incident Command is a safety critical function for all managers who have a responsibility to respond to incidents. It is essential that organisations are able to provide evidence that their ICs at all levels are competent and that the ICs themselves understand and maintain competence.

The key elements of the process are:

1.   The definition of competence
2.   National Occupational Standards
3.   Workplace Assessment
4.   Personal Development Records
5.   Continuing Personal Development (CPD)

It is important that the organisation and the individual are able to learn continuously from the successes and challenges experienced during Incident Command. Competence and the assessment of competence are fundamental to performance management, which states that if performance isn't being measured, it isn't being managed.

The process of the assessment of competence in terms of knowledge, skills, experience and understanding is explained below.

Throughout this manual, guidance is provided on good practice regarding Incident Command, however, it does not describe the significant professional knowledge and understanding needed to be able to apply ICS to different situations. The ability to do this consistently is the key and the introduction of the Integrated Personal Development System (IPDS) was brought in to achieve this.

At the very heart of IPDS is the term competence. IPDS supports competence by describing the systems that are necessary to ensure that UKFRS can be sure that its people are safe.

5.2   Definition of Competence

Competence is concerned with:

● outcomes, and the impact made upon performance,
● measurement against standards
● reviewing progress towards achieving the outcome; i.e. competent performance

Competence is the ability to consistently use knowledge, skills and understanding to the standards expected in employment, to meet changing demands and solve problems.

The features of occupational competence should encompass:

● Personal effectiveness – being able to get things done appropriately. It embraces the ability to successfully deal with situations and to interact with people employed in the workplace and being able to deal with contingencies as they arise, getting organised and getting results of the right quality in a reasonable time.

- A range of occupational skills – the skills, standards and practices associated with an occupation.
- The ability to transfer knowledge, skills and experience to situations e.g. experiences gained and utilised within other contexts.
- Personal qualities and attributes i.e. problem solving, planning and implementing (as per FSC 51/2004)

The Incident Commander will be operating within a risk environment that is possibly wide and complex, with many variables added by the actual situation being dealt with. The IC will have to satisfy four inter-related components; these are:

- Task skills, which are routine and largely technical components.
- Task management skills to manage a group of tasks and prioritise between them.
- Contingency management, which means the skills to recognise and deal with things that go wrong and with the unexpected.
- Role/job environmental skills, which are about ensuring safety, interacting with people and the ability to deal with the environmental factors required in fulfilling the wider role.

It is important that the individual is not only able to demonstrate adequately those physical skills involved in carrying out a range of tasks, but can manage a range of tasks at the same time. This must be done while planning contingency arrangements to cope if something goes wrong or there is an unexpected problem to solve. This must be achieved whilst considering the wider environmental issues and personal/interpersonal skills that are most appropriate to the situation.

5.3 National Occupational Standards

NOS are statements of the skills, knowledge and understanding needed in employment and clearly define the outcomes of competent performance. They are benchmarks of performance, providing the means for assessing performance in a job. In the early 1980s, the Government were determined to improve the effectiveness of British Industry by introducing national standards of occupational competence. These standards were to be 'explicit, agreed, widely accessible, flexible, progressive and testable' (Manpower Services Commission 1981). National Occupational Standards are concerned with what an individual can do, not just what they know.

The Qualifications and Curriculum Authority provides guidance that NOS should focus upon the critical aspects of competence at work. NOS can also be used for training, appraisals, recruitment, retention planning and Continuous Professional Development (CPD) needs.

The concept of assessing competence against (NOS) units, elements and the performance criteria can be a complex process.

Regarding Incident Command there are 3 separate standards that provide learning outcomes for the National Occupational Standards, listed opposite.

5.4 Unit

A unit of competence defines the broad functions carried out in a particular job role. It is the smallest sub-division of a key area of work.

As an example:

Lead, Monitor and Support people to resolve operational incidents (unit EFSM2). A unit describes a workplace activity that can be performed by a single person.

5.5 Element

Each unit is made up of at least two elements that provide a description of the main activities necessary for the completion of the unit. Therefore for Unit EFSM2, this unit comprises of 3 elements, i.e.

WM 7 Lead & Support people to resolve operational incidents	For those who respond to incidents in charge of fire appliances and crews (Crew Manager and Watch Manager)
	EFSM module database 008 describes the learning outcomes for those developing in this role

EFSM 2 Lead Support & Monitor people to resolve operational incidents	For those who respond to incidents of a more complex nature to support initial crews (Station, Group and Area Managers and also Brigade Managers who are required to assume tactical command at incidents)
	EFSM module database 027 describes the learning outcomes for those developing in this role

ESFM 1 Provide Strategic Advice and support to resolve operational incident	For those who respond to incidents to provide strategic advice and support (Area and Brigade Managers)
	EFSM module database 045 describes the learning outcomes for those developing in this role

2.1 Review and determine incident status.

2.2 Assume responsibility and implement action to support those involved in the incident.

2.3 Debrief following resolution of incident

The element is the sub-division of a unit of competence; it is a description of what a person should be able to do. It encompasses some action or outcome, having real meaning in the occupational sector to which it relates.

5.6 Performance Criteria

Each element of competence will have performance criteria, each of which consist of a short statement that has two components, a critical outcome and an evaluative statement. Successful achievement of an element will be recognised when the individual being assessed meets the stated performance criteria. As an example, see Section 5.13 Guidance for Assessors.

5.7 Knowledge and Understanding

This describes what must be known and understood and how this knowledge applies to the job. As an example, part of the knowledge for unit EFSM2 is:

- Role, responsibilities and level of authority at operational incidents
- Lines of communication at incidents and the incident command system

5.8 Workplace Assessment

Workplace assessment is a process for assessing people against NOS in the course of normal day to day activity. It helps to maintain skills, knowledge and understanding and provides evidence that people are competent. If there are shortfalls in performance these become part of the development required for the people concerned. To ensure that the assessment process is effective it is important to ensure that:

- Line managers/ assessors understand the requirements of the NOS
- A person's performance is judged against the NOS
- The nature and formats of assessment processes are known by those participating
- Opportunities that occur naturally in day to day work should be identified. Where this is not possible then appropriate Development Activities need to be constructed. For example, at the higher levels of Incident

Command, where naturally occurring opportunities are not available on a regular basis, then simulation could be used.

- People and assessors generate, collect and record relevant evidence to demonstrate competence
- Assessors make decisions and provide feedback
- Decisions and feedback are recorded

The assessor judges this evidence against all of the performance criteria and makes a decision that the standards have been met or that a development need has been identified.

5.9 Knowledge and Understanding in Incident Command

In order to function effectively, ICs must possess knowledge and understanding of the domain in which they are operating (and of the domains operating above and below). For example, to make an appropriate assessment of risk in a building, there must be an appreciation of building construction and the effects of a fire upon the structure. The IC must also be aware of the capabilities of the available resources in order to make an effective deployment.

An IC must consider many other factors, to varying degrees. A Crew Manager (CM) at a relatively small incident who is working at the operational level must have a highly detailed knowledge and understanding of the professional fire domain. Wider political or social implications factor less in the resolution of smaller scale incidents so while the CM must have an appreciation that these considerations exist, they need not concentrate too much on them.

In contrast, a Brigade Manager (BM), working at major incidents, possibly involving the strategic or 'Gold' level, must have a detailed understanding of the political, social and environmental implications that the incident may generate. The BM's specific domain knowledge and understanding does not need to be as technically detailed as that of the CM. For example, the BM in charge of a 25 pump fire does not need to know how to operate the pumps which are delivering the water to the incident, but does need to know the issues associated with reinstating normality for FRS and the business community.

Commanders at any level must also understand that all incidents have a wide impact. A car fire may have impacted upon the car's owner, who now has no car and cannot get to work. At the other end of the spectrum, a large fire at a factory making components for cars may result in the laying off of hundreds of workers. Incidents impact upon the natural environment; water run off can cause pollution that may persist for many years. Closure of a major transportation link as a result of an incident can have national economic implications.

A tactical or Silver Command Officer can be seen to need a different balance of all these skills. Although it can be argued that domain knowledge and understanding is of equal importance here, the officer working at this level has a significant level of support via the command team and Command Support and needs to begin to look outwards from the incident.

The comparison of the knowledge and understanding of the domain against the wider organisational considerations can be viewed as a sliding scale and is represented in the graph below.

Any overall judgement of competence should not be based upon one assessment only; it must be part of a process conducted over time. It is necessary to practice and be re-assessed, maintaining competence by Continuous Professional Development. More frequent assessment is needed for higher risk tasks and tasks where associated skills may decay more quickly.

5.10 Evidence

It is a basic principle of vocational competence that competence can only be demonstrated against the NOS, on several occasions and in various conditions and contexts. It therefore follows that evidence gathered to support the demonstration of competence during incident command must also be gathered according to:

● Observation of workplace activity
● Observation of simulated activity (Development Activities)

This may be supported by:

● Products of a person's work
● Witness testimony
● Personal statements
● Outcomes from questioning
● Debriefing

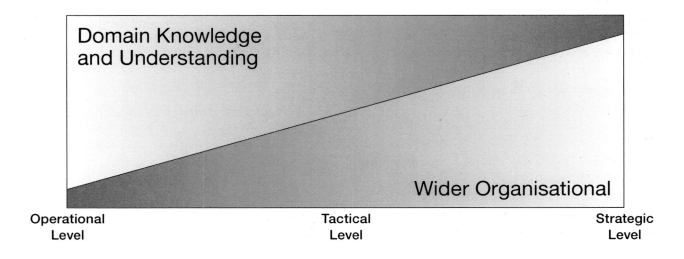

| Domain Knowledge and Understanding | | Wider Organisational |

| Operational Level | Tactical Level | Strategic Level |

In all cases regarding Incident Command, direct observation is crucial but can be supported by questioning or other means to explore the skills, knowledge, understanding and how, why and when the evidence was produced.

The Assessment Process

In most instances it will be line managers who will carry out workplace assessments, although they may also be completed by:

- Trainers at a training/development centre
- Other service assessors (e.g. observers at exercises/simulations)
- Other independent assessor's e.g. external organisations during Gold Command simulation exercises at the Fire Service College
- People with specialist skills who are qualified

Regardless of who carries out the assessment, all assessors must be familiar with the relevant NOS and suitably trained and competent to do so.

If the assessment is to gather evidence for a relevant qualification (S/NVQ) then the assessor must be qualified to do so.

Quality Assurance

FRSs should have in place a system that will ensure that the assessment process is fair and consistently applied. Question and answer sessions underpin workplace assessments and is one of eight components of IPDS. More information can be sourced in FSC 11/2003.

5.11 Personal Development Records

FRSs require a means by which they can:

- Record achievements
- Record competence
- Record development needs

Whichever system is adopted the following principles apply:

- A recording methodology is required to support the demonstration of competence and further development needs of people
- This methodology must complement the IPDS and withstand the scrutiny of audit (this is necessary to confer consistency and transferability across organisations)
- Systems should be non-bureaucratic and encourage people to feel that they 'own' their development
- The systems should inform the development planning process on a needs basis, for individual, teams or the organisation

5.12 Continuing Personal Development

Personal Development to meet the NOS and IPDS is a phased approach, incorporating:

- Acquisition of knowledge skills and understanding
- Application of knowledge skills and understanding in the workplace
- Maintenance of knowledge skills and understanding and CPD

It is important to note that in the wider personal context personnel may be in one or more phases in any point in their career. An individual may progress through the phases above as they change role and develop upwards adopting a different IC role on behalf of their organisations.

As the world around us changes and the core functions of FRSs widen, it is important that learning for ICs is designed to ensure that they can continue to operate competently within their current role.

CPD is an intrinsic part of Personal and Organisational Development (POD). Implementing effective CPD will give rise to both direct and indirect costs. FRSs should view this as an investment that may be expected to accrue savings over time. In particular the maintenance and further development of knowledge, skills and understanding through equitable development programmes will help organisations to:

- Support the safe person concept
- Meet duties under relevant law and regulations
- Meet the staff development implications of business risk management and organisational development policies

- Mitigate risk to the organisation from the potential occurrence of negligent acts
- Support fairness and equality policies
- Support national and European initiatives for life long learning
- Meet the requirements of quality assurance/ development initiatives, e.g. Investors in people (IIP), ISO 9000 etc.

5.13   Guidance for assessors

The following are provided as examples only.

Demonstration of competence against WM7.1
Example scenario:

A crew has been mobilised to a report of a fire at a vehicle repair workshop. Whilst mobile the crew could see a plume of smoke rising from the vicinity of the garage. Upon attendance, the crew were met by the occupier of the garage who stated that there was a car on fire inside the garage.

Performance Criteria	Example characteristics of an Incident Commander's performance which would meet the required standard
Collect and confirm information relevant to the known and anticipated risks to people, property and the environment	The Incident Commander discussed generic risks present in garage fires with the crew whilst mobile and asked the occupier whether all persons had been accounted for and about the presence of specific hazards such as acetylene cylinders, services, inspection pits, containers of fuel, materials which could be harmful to the environment, construction of the building, duration of the fire etc. Details of the hazards, such as location, quantity etc were confirmed with the occupier and the details were communicated to the crew members. The Incident Commander also considered wider implications such as previous incidents involving the same premises or other factors such as racial or other criminally motivated factors which may have led to the premises falling victim to arson.
Plan action to lead and support the crew's response to the incident	The Incident Commander devised and communicated a safe and effective plan of action, considering the requirement for any additional resources and taking into account the resources available and their skills. Clear briefings were given to crew members to enable them to understand exactly what they were required to do and that they were fully aware of the risks present in the premises.
Develop objectives through risk assessment	A DRA was conducted and objectives were planned in accordance with the DRA. The details of the DRA were communicated to all and a suitable Tactical Mode was declared and communicated to Control. Significant safety findings were recorded effectively.

Demonstration of competence against EFSM 2.1

Example scenario:

Four pumping appliances are in attendance at a fire in a vehicle repair workshop. The initial IC has implemented a tactical plan taking into account the information obtained from the occupier of the garage. The workshop contains an acetylene cylinder and there is an environmental hazard posed by the workshop asbestos roof. The Tactical Level IC has been mobilised to the incident.

Performance Criteria	Example characteristics of an Incident Commander's performance which would meet the required standard
Obtain sufficient information from all available sources on incident progress, risks, deployment, resource availability and existing incident management	The Tactical Level Incident Commander ensured that comprehensive additional information was obtained from Fire Control and through observation and consultation with the initial Incident Commander. This includes: Who are the Incident Commander and crew? Are they familiar with the locality and aware of any risks present? How experienced are the Incident Commander & crew? Have there been any previous incidents at this location? What possible causes are there for this incident – accidental through generic risks such as welding etc or deliberate through business competitors, disgruntled customer/employee? Could this be a crime scene? Are there any concerns over contamination from fire water run off? Will the incident cause severe traffic congestion? What time of day is it? Will customers be arriving to collect their cars? A comprehensive review of the tactical plan was undertaken taking into account all likely influencing factors. These include: Are safe systems of work employed? Are there sufficient numbers of suitable people available to perform the work? Are relief arrangements adequate? Are suitable rehydration and hygiene arrangements available? Has the use of specialist resources been considered fully? Resources in attendance and the effectiveness of their deployment were evaluated. This includes the number and skills of people already at the incident and who may be required. The existing Incident Command structure was thoroughly reviewed to ensure its effectiveness. The spans of control were evaluated to ensure the Incident Commander was not being overloaded with channels of direct communication. The use of sectorisation and functional roles was evaluated and implemented to delegate tasks efficiently.
Confirm that current action complies with relevant legislation and protocols	The Tactical Level Incident Commander carried out a comprehensive review of the tactics and ensured that the actions took into account the requirements of the FRSA 2004, Health & Safety at Work Act, environmental, Civil Contingencies Act and other relevant legislation. The Incident Commander demonstrated a thorough awareness and practical application of existing relevant risk information, procedures, 7.2 (d) information and GRAs and ensured these were implemented within the tactical plan.

Performance Criteria	Example characteristics of an Incident Commander's performance which would meet the required standard
Determine the current involvement of other agencies, their current activities and key contacts	The current and potential involvement of other Category 1 & 2 responders as defined in Parts 1 & 3 of Schedule 1 to the Civil Contingencies Act 2004. These include Police, Ambulance Service, Local Authority, Health Services, Utilities, Environment Agency, Environmental Health, Health Protection Agency, Highways Agency, etc. and any other relevant persons such as the premises occupier or owner was evaluated in full, taking into account wider implications of the incident such as: interruption to utility services, environmental pollution resulting from the incident, potential effect upon health in the area, preservation of evidence, disruption to transport infrastructure.

Demonstration of competence against EFSM 1

Example scenario: the collapse of a large public building in a city centre following an explosion.

Performance Criteria	Example characteristics of an Incident Commander's performance which would meet the required standard
1.1g anticipate the likely demand on resources and the implication overall service delivery	The strategic commander would arrange for ridership and appliance availability data for the next 48 hours to be made available immediately. Forecast rolling 20 pump, 10 officer peak requirement during the next 24 hours. Gather heads of department to analyse other known priority events in the next 2 working days and report back on their findings.
1.2f provide accurate and timely information to the media and utilise media resources to inform and protect the community	The strategic commander had a press conference arranged in liaison with other agencies involved and the known media contacts. Had a statement prepared in agreement with other agencies to inform and advise the community of the nature of the incident and possible short medium and long term effects.
1.2k conduct comprehensive and timely briefings with relevant people	The strategic commander initiated a conference briefing with the Chief Constable, Authority CEO, Authority party leaders and the Environment Agency Officer to outline the projected timeline of the incident to enable them to interface their interests, priorities and resources.

Appendices

APPENDIX 1
Analytical Risk Assessment Process

A1.1 Introduction

Having carried out a Dynamic Risk Assessment and established a Tactical Mode, the Incident Commander must consider a more detailed approach, this process is known in the FRS as the "Analytical Risk Assessment".

Due to the continually changing environment at an incident, for 'best practice' the IC should ensure that as soon as resources permit an ARA is performed and documented. This must be kept constantly under review and updated at 20 minute intervals or when ever the risk to crews changes.

A1.2 Analytical Risk Assessment Process

The Analytical Risk Assessment' includes the following elements:

- A formalised assessment of the hazards, who or what is at risk from those hazards, the likelihood and severity of risk

- An assessment of existing control measures with additional control measures introduced as appropriate
- Confirmation that the dynamic risk assessment and tactical mode was/is correct
- Informs ongoing DRA process

The Risk Management Model in figure A1 below is a tool that can be used on the incident ground to assist with the ARA process. It can also be used to feed relevant information from the incident ground, via the incident debrief, back into the risk assessment process at the systematic level, thereby confirming or amending the organisations 'Generic Risk Assessment' or the 'Standard Operational Procedures'.

Figure A2 is an example of an ARA form used at the Fire Service College. It is used in conjunction with the Generic Risk Assessments (GRA) found in "A Guide to Operational Risk Assessment" folder (Fire Service Guide Volume 3)

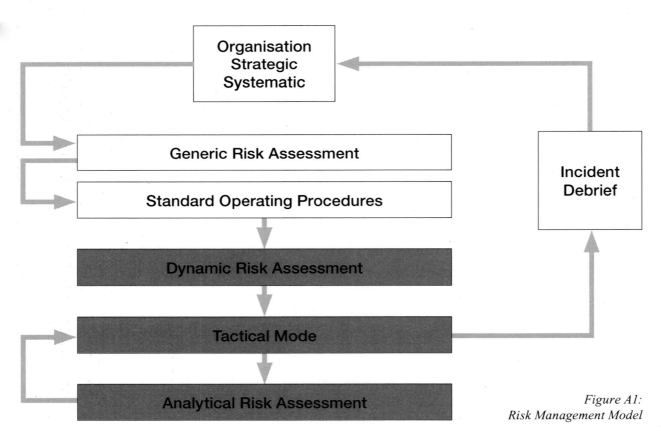

Figure A1: Risk Management Model

Example – Incident Ground Analytical Risk Assessment (ARA)

Incident Number .... Date & Time.............................. Sheet   of

Incident Type (GRA*) .... Address / Location .... Sector......

Hazards	Who is at risk?	Existing Control measures	S 1-5	L 1-5	S x L	Risk Rating	Are existing control measures adequate?	If NO – Implement additional control measures needed to reduce risk
Ensure ARA is updated at regular intervals								Continue on separate sheet if required

INCIDENT COMMANDER	FORM COMPLETED BY	PREVIOUS TACTICAL MODE
		CURRENT TACTICAL MODE

APPENDIX 1
Analytical Risk Assessment Process

Number	Incident Type – GRA*	Number	Incident Type – GRA*	Notes / Plans / Actions
	RESCUES		**TRANSPORT**	
2.1	Ice/unstable ground	4.1	Road	
2.2	Lifts and escalators	4.2	Rail	
2.3	Sewers	4.3	Air	
2.4	Silos	4.4	Marine	
2.5	Trench/pits		**GENERIC HAZARDS**	
2.6	Collapsed Structures	5.1	Electricity	
2.7	Height	5.2	Acetylene	
2.8	Flooding	5.3	Chemical	
2.9	Animals	5.4	Biological	
	FIGHTING FIRES	5.5	Confined Space	
3.1	Buildings	5.6	Civil disturbance	
3.2	High rises	5.7	Explosives	
3.3	Chimneys	5.8	Flashover/Backdraught	
3.4	Rural areas	5.9	Asbestos	
3.5	Farms			
3.6	Using PPV			
3.7	Refuse			
3.8	Public entertainment			
3.9	Secure accommodation		GRA* Generic Risk Assessments	
3.10	Petro chemical installations		found in a Guide to Ops. Risk	
3.11	Pipelines		*Assessment - Volume 3*	

Has the risk to the environment been considered? Y/N

Record any actions and control measures overleaf.

Where Risks are high or very high inform IC/SC immediately

Severity Rating (S)
1. INSIGNIFICANT – No injury
2. MINOR – First aid only
3. MODERATE – Hospital treatment required
4. SIGNIFICANT – Permanent disability/ Fatality
5. CATASTROPHIC – Multiple fatalities / Large-scale hospitalisation of casualties

Likelihood Rating (L)
1. RARE – May occur in exceptional circumstances
2. UNLIKELY – Will seldom occur
3. POSSIBLE – May occur
4. PROBABLE – Will often occur
5. HIGHLY PROBABLE – Near certain

S E V E R I T Y (S)		L=1	L=2	L=3	L=4	L=5
S	5	5	10	15	20	25
E	4	4	8	12	16	20
V	3	3	6	9	12	15
E	2	2	4	6	8	10
R	1	1	2	3	4	5
	(S)	1	2	3	4	5

LIKELIHOOD (L)

RISK	1-3 TOLERABLE No further action- monitor	4-8 MODERATE Reasonably satisfactory- minor actions required	9-14 HIGH Unsatisfactory - Immediate action required	15-25 VERY HIGH Unacceptable- take immediate action

A1.2.1 The Analytical Process

1. Complete the information surrounding the incident or sector and identify the appropriate GRA number if applicable (see reverse of form for index). Identify the significant hazards, those that may be at risk and the existing control measures.

2. Using the five-point grid to decide the SEVERITY and the LIKELIHOOD associated to each hazard. Multiply the severity and likelihood scores together and enter the total to calculate the risk rating: e.g. tolerable, moderate, high, very high.

3. Enter the total and the risk rating in the appropriate columns and decide if the existing control measures are adequate.

4. Where this is not the case, list additional controls measures that are necessary to make the management of the risk tolerable.

Any relevant notes or plans should be included on the rear of the form prior to it being signed by the Incident or Sector Commander taking responsibility for operations in the relevant area of operations.

Additional consideration should be given to environmental issues as soon as reasonably practicable,(the requirement to address this on the rear of the form should act as a prompt to IC or Sector Commander).

The completed forms should be collated by Command Support for debriefing and audit purposes.

APPENDIX 2
Incident Command System

Further Examples of Application of Sectorisation

Figure A2.1

Examples of Sector Development

Figure A2.2

Example of Sector Designation at a multiple RTC

Figure A2.3

Example of Tactical Mode, Hazardous substance release, Defensive Mode

Figure A2.4

Example of Tactical Mode, Hazardous substance release, Offensive Mode

Figure A2.5

Example of Tactical Mode, Hazardous substance release, Transitional

Figure A2.6

Example of Sectorisation for Ships.

Examples of Sector Development

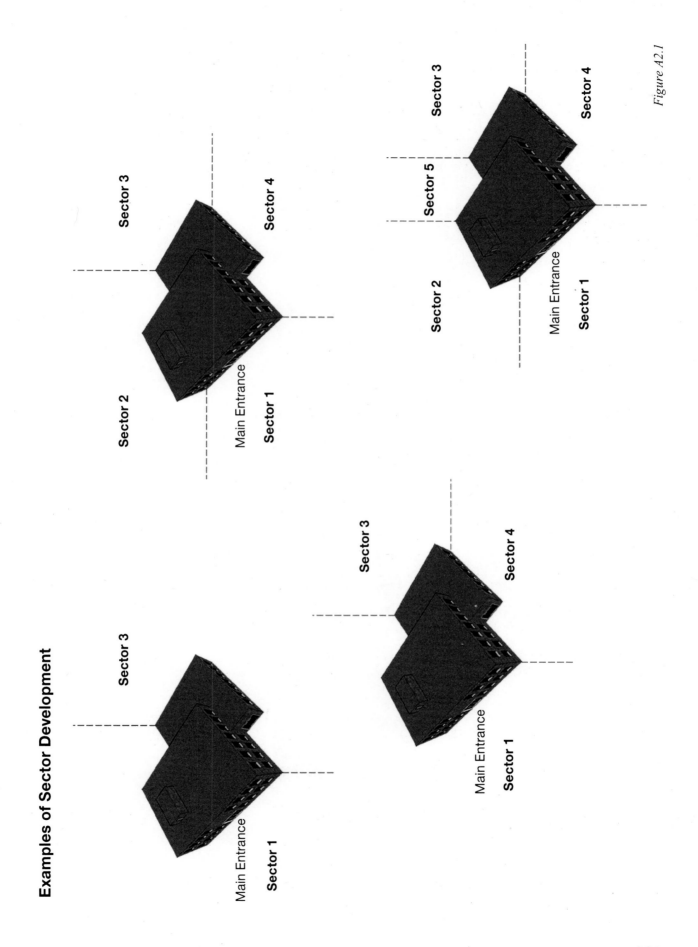

Figure A2.1

Example of Sector Designation at a multiple RTA

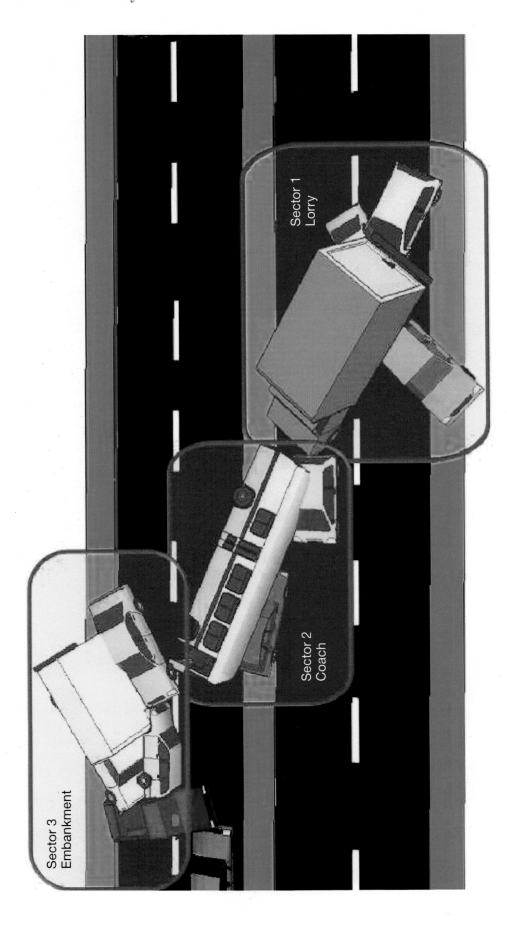

Sector 1
Lorry

Sector 2
Coach

Sector 3
Embankment

Figure A2.2

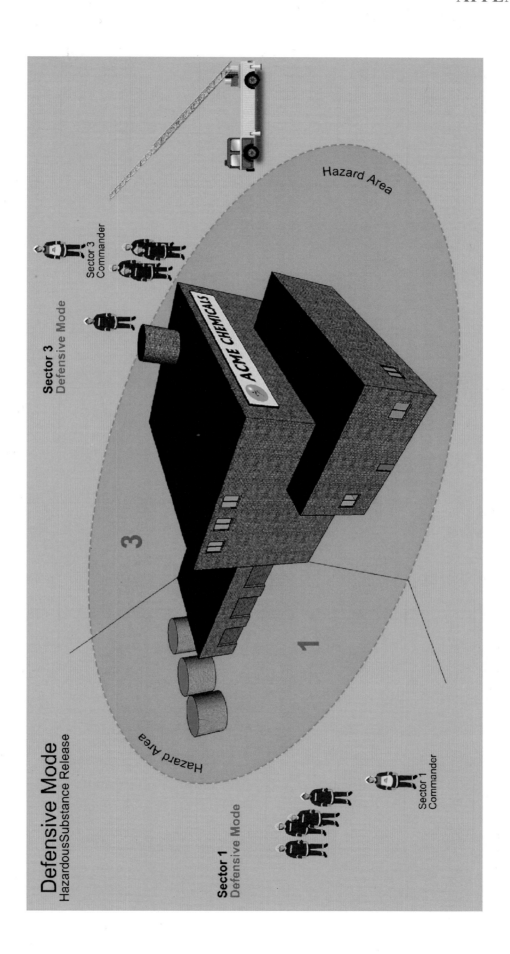

Defensive Mode
HazardousSubstance Release

Hazard Area

Sector 3
Defensive Mode

Sector 3
Commander

ACME CHEMICALS

Sector 1
Defensive Mode

Sector 1
Commander

Hazard Area

Figure A2.3

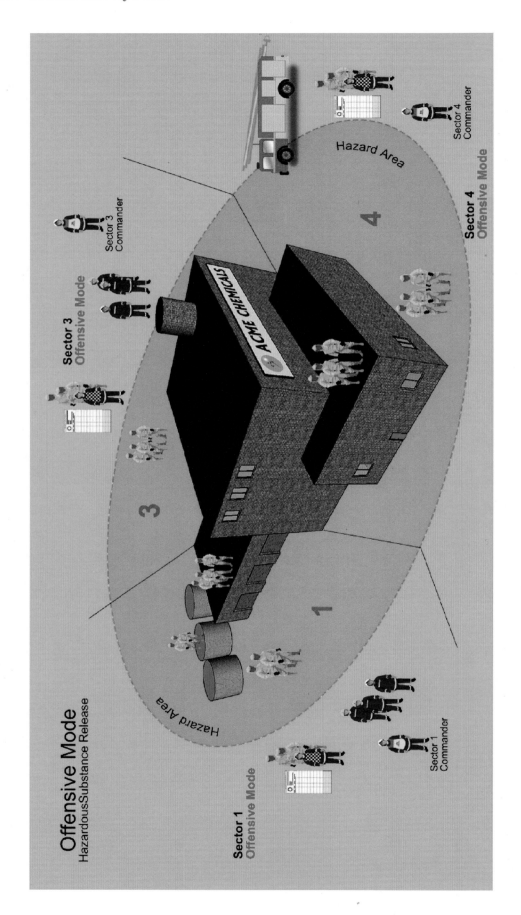

Figure A2.5

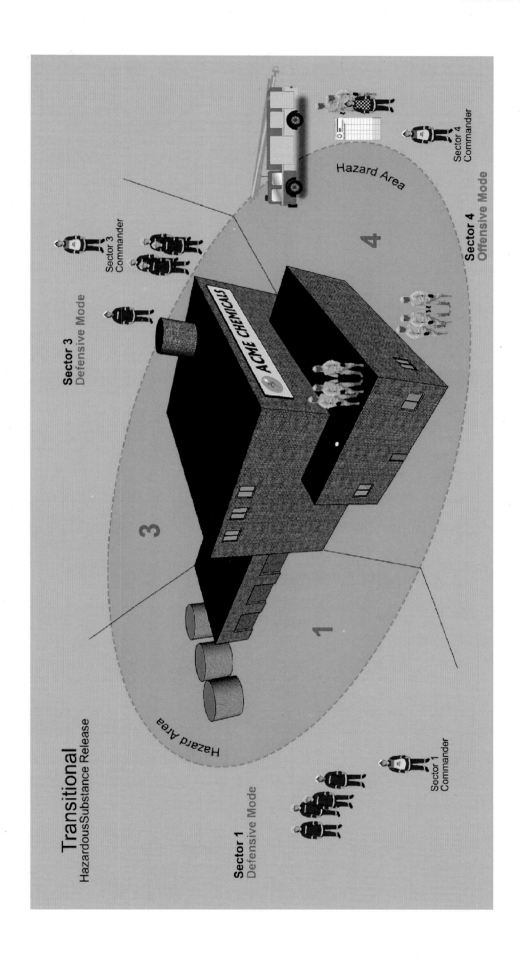

Transitional
HazardousSubstance Release

Sector 3
Defensive Mode

Sector 3
Commander

Sector 1
Defensive Mode

Sector 1
Commander

Hazard Area

Hazard Area

ACME CHEMICALS

3

1

4

Sector 4
Offensive Mode

Sector 4
Commander

Figure A2.6

Example of Sectorisation for Ships

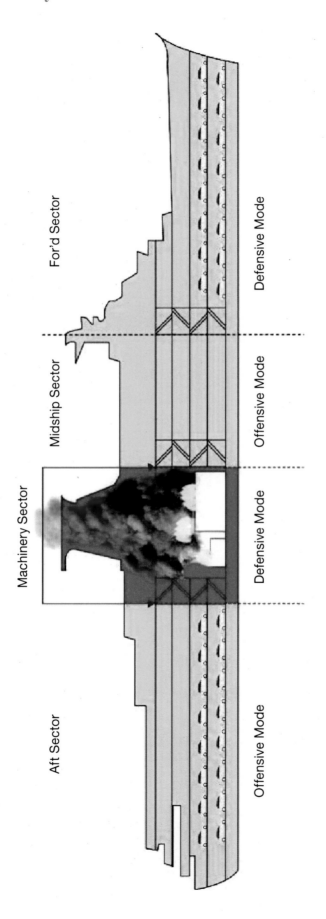

Figure A2.6

Aft Sector

Machinery Sector

Midship Sector

For'd Sector

Offensive Mode

Defensive Mode

Offensive Mode

Defensive Mode

APPENDIX 3
The Psychology of Command (courtesy of Professor Rhona Flin)

The psychology of command is beginning to emerge as a distinct research topic for psychologists interested in selection, training, competence assessment, decision making, stress management, leadership and team working. The following overview of recent research into decision making, stress and leadership is based on Flin (1996) which gives a more detailed examination of these issues.

A3.1 Decision Making

The decision making skill of the Incident Commander is one of the essential components of effective command and control in emergency response. Despite the importance of high speed decision making in the fire service and a number of other occupations, it has only been very recently that research psychologists have begun to investigate leaders' decision making in demanding, time-pressured situations.

The traditional decision-making literature from management, statistics and economics is very extensive but it offers little of relevance to the Incident Commander, as it tends to be derived from studies of specified problems (often artificial in nature), inexperienced decision makers and low stake payoffs. Moreover, it is rarely concerned with ambiguous, dynamic situations, life threatening odds or high time pressure, all important features of a fire or rescue environment.

If we turn to the standard psychological literature on decision-making it tells us almost nothing of emergency decision making, as so much of it is based on undergraduates performing trivial tasks in laboratories. Similarly, the management research is concerned with individuals making strategic decisions when they have several hours or days to think about the options, carefully evaluating each one in turn against their business objectives using decision analysis methods. These provide a range of explanatory frameworks, which may have value for managers' decision making where they are encouraged to emulate an analytical style of decision making. At its simplest form this usually incorporates the following stages:

1. Identify the problem.
2. Generate a set of options for solving the problem/choice alternatives.
3. Evaluate these options concurrently using one of a number of strategies, such as weighting and comparing the relevant features of the options.
4. Choose and implement the preferred option.

In theory, this type of approach should allow you to make the 'best' decision, provided that you have the mental energy, unlimited time and all the relevant information to carry out the decision analysis. This is typically the method of decision-making in which managers are trained. But we know from our everyday experience that when we are in a familiar situation, we take many decisions almost automatically on the basis of our experience. We do not consciously generate and evaluate options; we simply know the right thing to do. This may be called intuition or 'gut feel' but, in fact, to achieve these judgements some very sophisticated mental activity is taking place. So we can compare these two basic types of decision-making, the slower but more analytic comparison and the faster, intuitive judgement. Which style do commanders use when deciding what to do at the scene of an incident?

A3.2 Naturalistic Decision Making (NDM)

In the last ten years there has been a growing interest by applied psychologists into naturalistic decision making (NDM) which takes place in complex real world settings (Klein et al, 1993; Zsambok & Klein, 1997; Flin et al, 1997). These researchers typically study experts' decision making in dynamic environments such as flight decks, military operations, fire-grounds, hospital trauma centres/intensive care units and high hazard industries, for example nuclear plant control rooms. This NDM research has enormous significance for the understanding of how commanders and their teams make decisions at the scene of an incident as it offers descriptions of what expert commanders actually do when taking operational decisions in emergencies.

APPENDIX 3
The Psychology of Command

Ten factors characterise decision making in naturalistic settings:

1. Ill defined goals and ill structured tasks.
2. Uncertainty, ambiguity and missing data.
3. Shifting and competing goals.
4. Dynamic and continually changing conditions.
5. Action feedback loops (real-time reactions to changed conditions).
6. Time stress.
7. High Stakes.
8. Multiple players (team factors).
9. Organisational goals and norms.
10. Experienced decision makers

In typical NDM environments information comes from many sources, is often incomplete, can be ambiguous, and is prone to rapid change. In an emergency, the Incident Commander and her or his team are working in a high stress, high risk, time pressured setting and the lives of those affected by the emergency, (including their own fire rescue personnel) may be dependent on their decisions.

How then do they decide the correct courses of action? In the view of the NDM researchers, traditional, normative models of decision making which focus on the process of option generation and simultaneous evaluation to choose a course of action do not frequently apply in NDM settings. There are a number of slightly different theoretical approaches within the NDM fraternity to studying decision making but they all share an interest in dynamic high pressure domains where experts are aiming for satisfactory rather than optimal decisions due to time and risk constraints.

A3.3   Recognition-Primed Decision Making (RPD)

Dr Gary Klein of Klein Associates, Ohio, conducts research into decision making by attempting to 'get inside the head' of decision makers operating in many different domains. Klein's approach stemmed from his dissatisfaction with the applicability of traditional models of decision making to real life situations, particularly when the decisions could

be lifesaving. He was interested in operational environments where experienced decision makers had to determine a course of action under conditions of high stakes, time pressures, dynamic settings, uncertainty, ambiguous information and multiple players.

Klein's research began with a study of urban fire-ground commanders who had to make decisions such as whether to initiate search and rescue, whether to begin an offensive attack or concentrate on defensive precautions and how to deploy their resources (Klein et al, 1986) They found that the fireground commanders' accounts of their decision making did not fit in to any conventional decision-tree framework.

"The fire ground commanders argued that they were not 'making choices', 'considering alternatives' or 'assessing probabilities'. They saw themselves as acting and reacting on the basis of prior experience; they were generating, monitoring and modifying plans to meet the needs of the situations. Rarely did the fire ground commanders contrast even two options. We could see no way in which the concept of optimal choice might be applied. Moreover it appeared that a search for an optimal choice could stall the fire ground commanders long enough to lose control of the operation altogether. The fire ground commanders were more interested in finding actions that were workable, timely and cost-effective." (Klein et al, 1993, p139).

During post-incident interviews, they found that the commanders could describe other possible courses of action but they maintained that during the incident they had not spent any time deliberating about the advantages or disadvantages of these different options.

It appeared that these Incident Commanders had concentrated on assessing and classifying the situation in front of them. Once they recognised that they were dealing with a particular type of event, they usually also knew the typical response to tackle it. They would then quickly evaluate the feasibility of that course of action, imagining how they would implement it, to check whether anything important might go wrong. If they envisaged any problems, then the plan might be modified but only if they rejected it, would they consider another strategy.

Klein Associates have also studied other decision makers faced with similar demand characteristics (e.g. tank platoon captains, naval warfare commanders, intensive care nurses) and found the same pattern of results. On the basis of these findings they developed a template of this strategy called the Recognition-Primed Decision Model. This describes how experienced decision makers can rapidly decide on the appropriate course of action in a high-pressure situation.

The model has evolved into three basic formats (see Figure A 3/1).

In the simplest version, shown as Level 1, the decision maker recognises the type of situation, knows the appropriate response and implements it.

If the situation is more complex and/or the decision maker cannot so easily classify the type of problem faced, then as in Level 2, there may be a more pronounced diagnosis (situation assessment) phase. This can involve a simple feature match where the decision maker thinks of several interpretations of the situation and uses key features to determine which interpretation provides the best match with the available cues. Alternatively, the decision maker may have to combine these features to construct a plausible explanation for the situation; this is called story building, an idea that was derived from legal research into juror decision-making. Where the appropriate response is unambiguously associated with the situation assessment it is implemented as indicated in the Level 1 model.

In cases where the decision maker is less sure of the option, then the RPD model, Level 3 version indicates that before an action is implemented there is a brief mental evaluation to check whether there are likely to be any problems. This is called mental simulation or pre-playing the course of action

(an 'action replay' in reverse) and if it is deemed problematical then an attempt will be made to modify or adapt it before it is rejected. At that point the commander would re-examine the situation to generate a second course of action.

Key features of the RPD model are as follows:

- Focus on situation assessment
- Aim is to satisfy not optimise
- For experienced decision makers, first option is usually workable
- Serial generation and evaluation of options (action plans)
- Check action plan will work using mental simulation
- Focus on elaborating and improving action plan
- Decision maker is primed to act

To the decision maker, the NDM type strategies (such as RPD) feel like an intuitive response rather than an analytic comparison or rational choice of alternative options. As 'intuition' is defined as, "the power of the mind by which it immediately perceives the truth of things without reasoning or analysis" then this may be an acceptable label for RPD which is rapid situation assessment to achieve pattern recognition and associated recall of a matched action plan from memory.

At present this appears to be one of the best models available to apply to the emergency situation whether the environment is civilian or military; onshore or offshore; aviation, industrial, or medical. In the USA, the RPD model is being widely adopted, it is being used at the National Fire Academy as well as in a number of military, medical, aviation and industrial settings (see Klein, 1998). The RPD model and associated research techniques have begun to generate a degree of interest in the UK, most notably by the Defence Research Agency and the Fire Service.

APPENDIX 3
The Psychology of Command

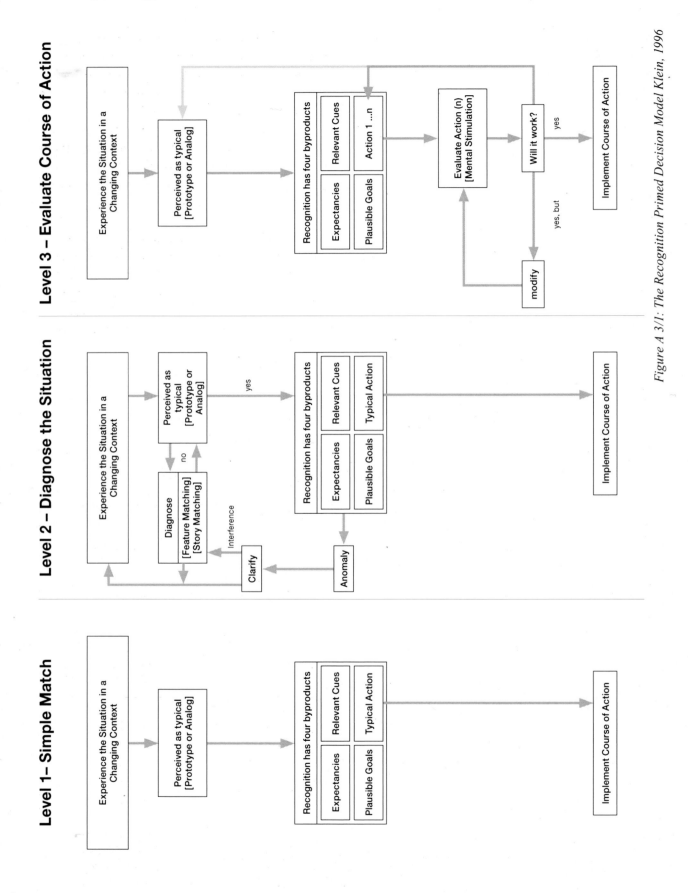

Figure A 3/1: The Recognition Primed Decision Model Klein, 1996

A3.4 Command roles and decision style

Obviously the RPD approach is not appropriate for all types of operational decisions and other NDM researchers have been developing taxonomies of the different types of decisions other emergency commanders, such as pilots, make in different situations (see Figure A3/2). The NASA Crew Factors researchers (Orasanu, 1995) have found that two key factors of the initial situation assessment are judgements of time and risk and that these may determine the appropriate decision strategy to use. The issue of dynamic risk analysis is a significant component of situation assessment on the fireground as discussed in Chapter 3 (see also Fire Engineers Journal, May, 1998).

If we consider the Orasanu model, the key skill is matching the correct decision style to the demands or allowances of the situation. For example, not using the fast intuitive RPD style when there is time to evaluate options. Furthermore senior fire officers in strategic command roles may require special training to discourage them from using the fast RPD approach when a slower, analytical method would be more appropriate (Fredholm, 1997).

There are significant differences in the balance of cognitive skills required of commanders, depending on their role (rather than rank) in a given operation, ascending from operational or task level, to tactical command, and to strategic command (Home Office, 1997). From studies of

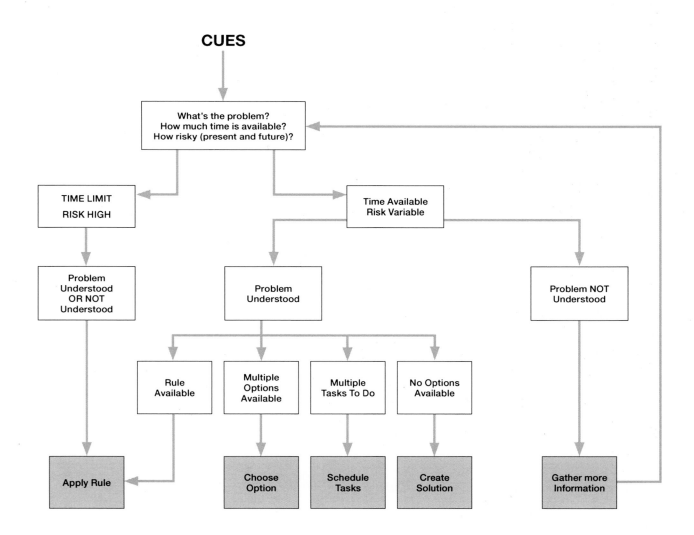

commanders' decision strategies (see Flin, 1996; Flin et al, 1997; Zsambok & Klein, 1997) these roles are briefly outlined below in terms of the decision skills required.

The figure below shows the decision process model for fixed wing pilots. (Orasanu 1995B) Reprinted with permission of the Human Factors and Ergonomics Society

Strategic Command

This involves the overall policy of command and control, deciding the longer term priorities for tactical commanders and planning for contingencies depending on the enemy's response. The task also contains a strong analytical element, as co-ordination of multiple sources of information and resources demands an awareness that cannot be based on procedures alone.

The decision making style assumed to be adopted for strategic decision making is creative or analytical, since the situations encountered will feature a number of novel elements or developments the strategic commander has not previously encountered.

Neither time pressure nor high immediate risk should be influencing command at this level, where the aim, if possible, is to devise an optimal solution for the situation, taking into account the wider and longer term implications. The strategic commander is usually remote from the incident and will be supported throughout by a team of lower ranking officers.

Tactical Command

This refers to the planning and co-ordination of the actions determined at the strategic level.

Due to the higher time pressure at this level, decision-making is based to a much greater extent on condition action matching, or rule-based reasoning. This style is characterised by controlled actions derived from procedures stored in memory. Control of behaviour at this level is goal oriented

and structured by 'feed-forward control' through a stored rule. Stored rules are of the type if (state) then (diagnosis) or if (state) then (remedial action).

The tactical decision maker is likely to be on scene, with a remit to maintain a good mental model of the evolving plan and unfolding events. Situation assessment is expected to be a more significant component of tactical decision-making than spending time choosing appropriate responses. However the tactical commander may have to 'create' time to engage in reflective thinking and when necessary to use more analytic decision strategies to evaluate alternative courses of action.

Kerstholt (1997, p189) found from an interview study with battalion commanders of peace-keeping operations, that, "decisions were mostly made analytically in the planning phase and intuitively during the execution of the mission. By analytic procedure we meant that several options were explicitly weighed against each other, whereas an intuitive decision meant that the commander immediately 'knew' which decision to take."

Operational Command

This involves front line or sector commanders who have to implement orders from the tactical level. They are operating in real time and have to react rapidly to situational demands. Decision making at this level is assumed to contain rule-based and intuitive elements. It is assumed that under time pressure and at high risk, they primarily make decisions based on pattern recognition (e.g. RPD) of the situations encountered. Ongoing situation awareness must remain very high as their performance depends on rapid identification of the situation and fast access to stored patterns of pre-programmed responses.

Only when time permits will they be able to engage in analytic decision making and option comparison. Striving to find optimal solutions runs the risk of 'stalling' their decision making, therefore their main objective is to find a satisfactory, workable course of action.

A3.5 Styles of Command Decision Making

From the above description of decision making techniques associated with particular command roles, there appear to be four main styles of decision making used by commanders: creative, analytical, procedural and intuitive.

The most sophisticated (and resource intensive) is creative problem solving which requires a diagnosis of an unfamiliar situation and the creation of a novel course of action. This is the most demanding of the four techniques, requires significant expertise and as Kersholt (1997) found, is more likely to be used in a planning phase rather than during an actual operation.

Analytical decision making also requires a full situation assessment, rigorous information search and then recall, critical comparison and assessment of alternative courses of action. Again with proper preparation, some of these option choices may already have been evaluated during exercises or planning meetings. These are the two most powerful decision techniques as they operate on large information sets but consequently they require far greater cognitive processing. Thus, they take a longer time to accomplish, and for most individuals can only be used in situations of relative calm and minimal distraction.

In fast moving, high-risk situations these styles are difficult if not impossible to use, and in order to maintain command and control, officers have to rely on procedural or intuitive styles which will produce a satisfactory, if not an optimal decision.

Procedural methods involve the identification of the problem faced and the retrieval from memory of the rule or taught method for dealing with this particular situation. Such decision methods (e.g. drills, routines and standard procedures) are frequently practised in training.

With experience, officers may also use the fastest style of decision making, intuitive or recognition-primed decision making described above. In this case there may not be a written rule or procedure but the commander rapidly recognises the type of situation and immediately recalls an appropriate course of action, on the basis of prior experience.

Decision Style	Cognitive Processes
Creative Problem Solving	Diagnosis of unfamiliar situation requiring extensive information search and analysis. Development/synthesis of new courses of action. Knowledge-based reasoning.
Analytical Option Comparison	Retrieval and comparison of several courses of action. High working memory load. Knowledge-based reasoning.
Procedural/ Standard Operating Procedures	Situation identification. Retrieval (and rehearsal) of rules for course of action Explicit rule-based reasoning. If x then y.
Intuitive/ Recognition-primed decisions (RPD)	Rapid situation recognition based on pattern matching from long-term memory. Implicit rule based or skill-based. 'Gut feel'

Table 1: Command decision styles

APPENDIX 3
The Psychology of Command

The evidence suggests that commanders use all four decision styles to a greater or lesser degree depending on the event characteristics and resulting task demands. For more senior commanders, distanced from the front line, the task characteristics change in terms of time frame, scale, scope and complexity, necessitating greater use of analytical and creative skills (Fredholm, 1997).

Studies of military and aviation commanders have shown that the following factors are of particular significance in determining decision style:

● available time
● level of risk
● situation complexity/familiarity,(or none at all)
● availability of information

The training implications of applying this new decision research to fire and rescue operations is first to determine the types of situations where experienced fire commanders use the intuitive RPD type of decision making. In these situations the critical focus will be on situation assessment. So the next stage is to discover the cues these experts use when quickly sizing up an incident and the responses they would choose to apply once they have assessed the situation.

Less experienced commanders need to be trained to recognise the key features or cues of different scenarios using simulated incidents with detailed feedback on their decision making. They need to develop a store of incident memories (from real events, simulator training, case studies, expert accounts) which they can use to drive their search for the critical classifying information at a new incident.

The US Marines who favour the RPD model have developed a very useful volume of 15 decision exercises in Mastering Tactics: A Tactical Decision Games Workbook (Schmitt, 1994, see Klein, 1998). These are a series of tactical decision scenarios where a description of a problem is presented and officers are required to quickly work out and explain a solution to the problem which can then be discussed with the team and/or the trainer. This assists officers to learn the critical cues for given types of situations and to store methods of dealing with new situations.

In essence the basis of good command training must be a proper understanding of the decision making processes utilised by effective commanders.

Psychologists can offer a range of research techniques to begin to explore in a more scientific fashion the skills of incident command (e.g. Burke, 1997; Flin et al, 1997). For instance, one of the most salient features of a fireground commander's decision task is the speed of fire development. Brehmer (1993) is particularly interested in this type of dynamic decision task, which he believes has four important characteristics: a series of decisions which are interdependent, a problem which changes autonomously, and as a result of the decision maker's actions, and a real time scenario.

He gives the following example, "Consider the decision problems facing a fire chief faced with the task of extinguishing forest fires. He receives information about fires from a spotter plane and on the basis of this information, he then sends out commands to his firefighting units. These units then report back to him about their activities and locations as well as about the fire and the fire chief uses this information (and whatever other information he may be able to get, e.g., from a personal visit to the fire and the fire fighting units) to issue new commands until the fire has been extinguished." (p1).

Brehmer and his colleagues have developed a computer programme (FIRE) based on a forest fire scenario which incorporates the four elements of dynamic decision making described above. The decision maker takes the role of the fire chief and using the grid map of the area shown on the computer screen, she or he has to make a series of decisions about the deployment of fire fighting resources with the goal of extinguishing the fire and protecting a control base.

The commander's actions are subject to feedback delays, that is time delay in actions being implemented or in the commander receiving status update information. Brehmer's studies have shown that decision makers frequently do not take such feedback delays into account, for example sending out too few firefighting units because they do not anticipate that the fire will have spread by the time they receive the status report.

He argues that the decision maker needs to have a good 'mental model' of the task in order to control a dynamic event, such as a forest fire, and his research has enabled him to identify several problems of model formation: dealing with complexity, balancing competing goals, feedback delays and taking into account possible side effects of actions. Brehmer (1993) uses control theory to encapsulate the dynamic decision process, "the decision maker must have clear goals, he must be able to ascertain the state of the system that he seeks to control, he must be able to change the system, and he must have a model of the system.," (p 10).

A3.6 Causes of Stress for Commanders

In fireground operations, stress may also have an impact on commanders' decision making and techniques for managing this need to be considered (see Flin 1996 for further details).

The effects of stress on commanders' thinking and decision making ability are of particular interest. Charlton (1992) who was responsible for the selection of future submarine commanders referred to the 'flight, fight or freeze' response manifested as problems in decision making, 'tunnel vision', misdirected aggression, withdrawal, and the 'butterfly syndrome' "where the individual flits from one aspect of the problem to another, without method solution or priority" (p54). He also mentions self delusion where the student commander denies the existence or magnitude of a problem, regression to more basic skills, and inability to prioritise.

Weiseath (1987) discussing the enhanced cognitive demands for leaders under stress describes reduced concentration, narrowing of perception, fixation, inability to perceive simultaneous problems, distraction, difficulty in prioritising and distorted time perception.

Brehmer (1993) argues that three 'pathologies of decision making' can occur, he calls these

I.   thematic vagabonding when the decision maker shifts from goal to goal
II. encystment the decision maker focuses on only one goal that appears feasible, and as in (i) fails to consider all relevant goals; and
III. a refusal to make any decisions.

Not all researchers agree that the decision making of experienced Incident Commanders will be degraded by exposure to acute stressors. Klein (1998) points out that these effects are most typical when analytical decision strategies are used,. In contrast, the recognition-primed type of decision strategy employed by experts under pressure may actually be reasonably stress-proof.

A3.7 Leadership

Leadership ability is generally deemed to be a key attribute of an Incident Commander and to some extent may be regarded as an umbrella term for the required competencies which have to be trained. However, finding a precise specification of the required behaviours or the style of leadership is rather less frequently articulated.

Leadership within a military context embodies the concepts of command, control, organisation and duty. There has been extensive military research into leadership much of which unfortunately never sees the light of day outside the defence research community.

APPENDIX 3
The Psychology of Command

The dominant model of leadership for training in the British armed services, the emergency services and in lower level management is Adair's (1988) Action Centred Leadership with its simple three circles model.

Adair developed his ideas from his experiences with the British Army, and he maintained that the effective leader must focus on the needs of the individual, the task and the team. This functional model has not changed significantly since its initial exposition thirty years ago and continues to be taught in a wide range of management courses. While the three circles diagram and the associated advice to leaders is intuitively appealing, there has been little empirical work to test whether it can actually function as an explanatory theory of leadership in routine managerial duties or emergency command situations.

The managerial research literature on leadership is a progression from a long standing focus on leadership characteristics, to research in the 1960s on leader behaviours (e.g. autocratic vs democratic; team vs task), to an awareness that "one size fits all" recommendations of the best leadership style are unlikely to work. The contingency theories emphasised that leadership style cannot be considered in isolation. Thus, what is effective leadership behaviour is likely to be dependent on the leader's personality and skills, the situation and the competence and motivation of the group being led. Thus the most effective leader needs to:

I.   be able to diagnose the situation (the task/problem, the mood, competence, motivation of the team),
II. have a range of styles available (e.g. delegative, consultative, coaching, facilitating, directive),
III. match her or his style to the situation (for example Hersey and Blanchard's (1988) model of situational leadership).

In an emergency which has high time pressure and risk, then it is unlikely that a consultative leadership style would be totally appropriate and while the Incident Commander needs to solicit advice from available experts and to listen to the sector commanders, the appropriate style is likely to be closer to directive than democratic.

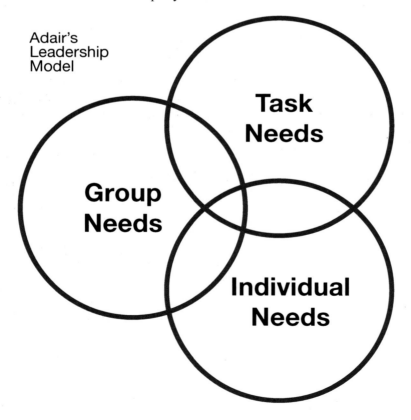

Adair's Leadership Model

Task Needs

Group Needs

Individual Needs

The need for a perceptible change in leadership style is very obvious when observing simulated emergency exercises when the time pressure and task demands are increased. Moreover, this sends a very important message to the rest of the team that the situation is serious and that they will also have to 'change gear' and sharpen their performance.

Within the business world, the current fashions in leadership style are the delegative, consultative styles, couched in the language of empowerment and transformational leadership. These approaches have not been developed with the Incident Commander in mind and while it was argued above that a consultative style may be inappropriate, particularly in the opening stages of an incident, this does not mean that there should be no delegation to more junior commanders.

In a larger incident considerable authority has to be devolved to sector commanders who will be required to take critical decisions and who will not always have time or opportunity to seek the opinion of the Incident Commander. These individuals need to have the expertise and the confidence to make decisions as the need arises.

The essential point is that the commander should be comfortable with the style required and that the front-line commanders should have a clear understanding of their delegated authority and the Incident Commander's plan of action.

Finally, the Incident Commander does not, and should not work alone. The need for effective team performance on the incident ground remains paramount. Recent advances in team training, known as Crew Resource Management (CRM) have been developed by the aviation industry and are now used in medicine and the energy industry. The focus is on non-technical skills relevant to incident command, such as leadership, situation awareness, decision making, team climate and communication (see Flin, 1995b; Salas et al, in press for further details). Fire officers who have studied this particular type of human factors training have argued that it has clear applications for the fire service (Bonney, 1995, Wynne, 1994).

References to Appendix Three

Brunacini, A. (1991) Command safety: A wake-up call. National Fire Protection Association Journal, January, 74-76.

Burke, E. (1997) Competence in command: Research and development in the London Fire Brigade. In R. Flin, E. Salas, M. Strub & L. Martin (Eds) Decision Making under Stress. Aldershot: Ashgate.

Driskell, J. & Salas, E. (1996) (Eds) Stress and Human Performance. Mahwah, NJ: LEA.

Flin, R. (1995a) Incident command: Decision making and team work. Journal of the Fire Service College, 1, 7-15.

Flin, R. (1995b) Crew Resource Management for teams in the offshore oil industry. Journal of European Industrial Training, 19,9, 23-27.

Flin, R. (1996) Sitting in the Hot Seat. Leaders and Teams for Critical Incident Management. Chichester: Wiley.

Flin, R., Salas, E., Strub, M. & Martin, L. (1997) (Eds) Decision Making under Stress: Emerging Themes and Applications. Aldershot: Ashgate.

Fredholm, L. (1997) Decision making patterns in major fire-fighting and rescue operations. In R. Flin, E. Salas, M. Strub & L. Martin (Eds) Decision Making under Stress. Aldershot: Ashgate.

Home Office (1997) Dealing with Disaster. Third edition. London: TSO

Klein, G. (1998) Sources of Power How People Make Decisions. Cambridge, Mass: MIT Press.

APPENDIX 3
The Psychology of Command

Klein, G. (1997) The Recognition-Primed Decision (RPD) model: Looking back, looking forward. In C. Zsambok & G. Klein (Eds) Naturalistic Decision Making. Mahwah, NJ: Lawrence Erlbaum.

Klein, G., Calderwood, R., & Clinton-Cirocco, A. (1986) Rapid decision making on the fireground. In Proceedings of the Human Factors Society 30th Annual Meeting. San Diego: HFS.

Klein, G., Orasanu, J., Calderwood, R. & Zsambok, C. (1993). (Eds.) Decision Making in Action. New York: Ablex.

Murray, B. (1994) More guidance needed for senior commanders on the fireground. Fire, 87, June, 21-22.

Orasanu, J. & Fischer, U. (1997) Finding decisions in naturalistic environments: The view from the cockpit. In C. Zsambok & G. Klein (Eds) Naturalistic Decision Making. Mahwah, NJ: LEA.

Salas, B., Bowers, C. & Edens, B. (in press) (eds.) Applying Resource Management in Organisations. New Jersey. LEA.

Schmitt, J. (1994) Mastering Tactics. Tactical Decision Game Workbook. Quantico, Virginia. US Marine Corps Association.

Zsambok, C. & Klein, G. (1997) (Eds) Naturalistic Decision Making. Mahwah, NJ: LEA.

APPENDIX 4
Decision Making Model (courtesy of London Fire Brigade)

1.   Introduction

1.1   This note introduces the Decision Making Model as a tool for Dynamic Risk Assessment (DRA). The model provides a framework for decision making for any task or event, every individual requires the skills to apply its principles in order to control the risks associated with an activity. The Decision Making Model is therefore applicable to **all** Personnel at all levels.

1.2   This guidance discusses the various stages of the Decision Making Model and explains how the process achieves DRA.

1.3   The cyclical nature of the model means that it is particularly suitable for changing and dynamic environments. The model is a simple flow diagram which guides users through the decision making process in an organised way. This process reduces the potential for information to be missed and requires objectives to be set and implemented. A key element in this process is the **consideration of safety** and the **development of safe systems of work**.

Application of the Decision Making Model for Personal Development

1.4   This system clearly identifies best practice in decision making for all personnel developing these skills. Formalising a best practice approach to Decision Making facilitates consistent feedback to individuals on their performance and identifies both positive and negative aspects of their actions. Some of the benefits of this are listed below:

To the individual:
- Encourages individuals to use their initiative and take personal responsibility.
- Facilitates consistent assessment of management skills.
- Brings together and reinforces training and actual experience.
- Provides a structure for developing and controlling safe systems of work.

To the Service:
- Identifies areas for further in-depth analysis and review.
- Supports the training of officers in the management process.

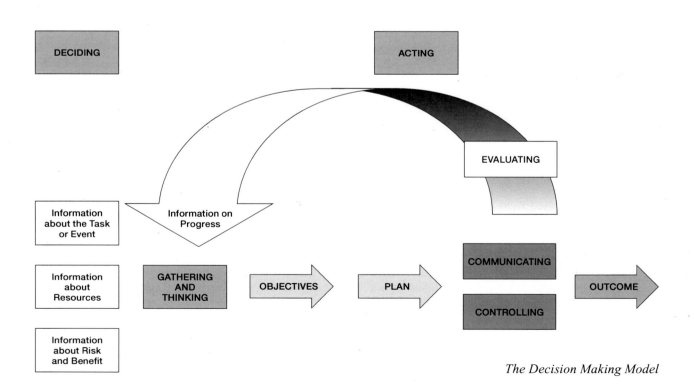

The Decision Making Model

APPENDIX 4
Decision Making Model

- Improves the knowledge and skills of any personnel who may undertake the role of manager at any level.

1.5 Use of the Decision Making Model will confirm best practice and identify training needs when applied to a dynamic situation. The feedback process will also identify when policy, procedures or equipment need to be introduced or improved.

1.6 The following are examples of when the decision making model could benefit personnel other than those attending operational incidents. The list is not exhaustive:

- Accidents, accident investigation and post accident action.
- Performance or conduct issues.
- Compliments or complaints procedures.
- Welfare issues.

2. The Decision Making Model

2.1 The Decision Making Model is formed around two main activities, Deciding and Acting. Each stage identified in the model falls into one of these activities.

Deciding
- Gathering and thinking about all available information.
- Identifying appropriate objectives.
- Defining a plan.
- Considering the results of evaluations.

Acting
- Communicating the objectives and plan to all those at the incident.
- Controlling the activity.
- Evaluating the outcome of the plan.

2.2 The functions within the two main activities of the Decision Making Model are explained as follows.

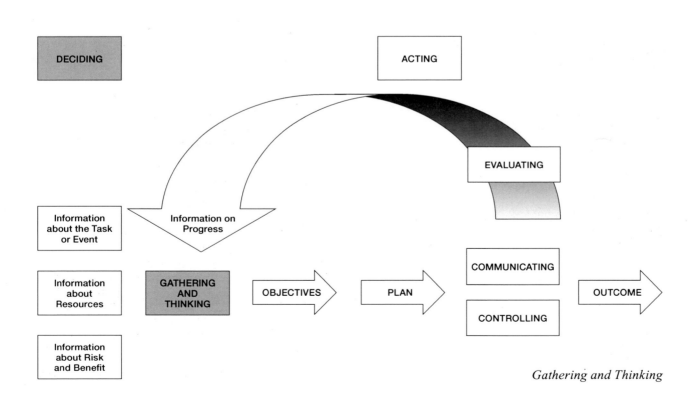

Gathering and Thinking

Gathering and Thinking

2.3   It is often not possible to gather all of the information about a task or event before it is necessary to take action.

2.4   In seeking to achieve safe systems of work it is vital that sufficient information is gathered upon which a reasoned decision can be made.

2.5   In order to achieve safe systems, a key factor will be the nature of the task or event and the time pressures that are associated with it.

3.   Information Gathering

3.1   During the initial stages of any decision making process it is necessary to gather relevant information. There are four sources of information that should be considered:

- Information of the Task/Event.
- Information on Resources.
- Information on Risks and Benefits.
- Information on Progress.

3.2   This links with *Step 1 of the Dynamic Risk Assessment:*

Evaluation of the situation, task and persons at risk.

4.   Information about the task or event

4.1   The first stage in the process involves gathering relevant information, whilst making the best use of the time available. It must be recognised that information gathering is the key to effective decision making.

4.2   The following are some examples of information about the Task/Event that the person or persons following the process should be considering.

- What is the environment?
- What is happening?
- Is the situation static of developing.
- What was it that led up to the event?
- Who is involved?
- Are there any immediate risks to anyone?

This list is not exhaustive and other information available may prove vital to the decision making process.

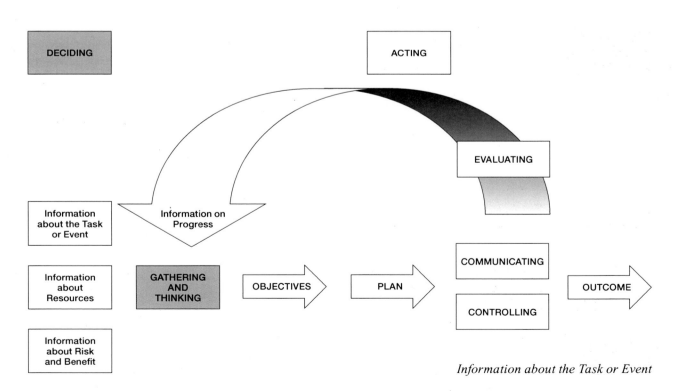

Information about the Task or Event

APPENDIX 4
Decision Making Model

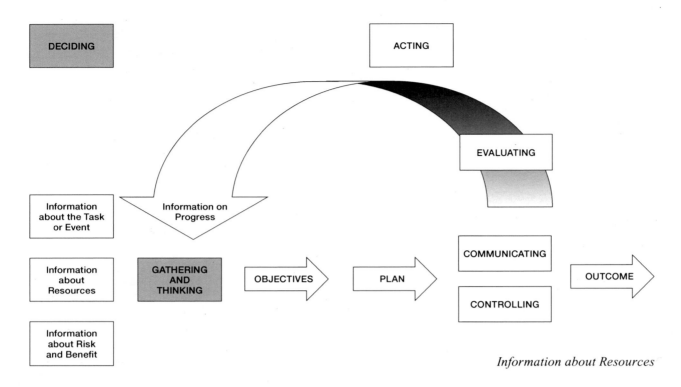

Information about Resources

5. Information about available resources

5.1   What is available to assist in the resolution of the task or event? This may include:

● People
● Equipment.
● Agreed policies and procedures.
● Information sources.
● Other agencies and knowledge or training.

The list may be extensive depending on the complexity of the situation.

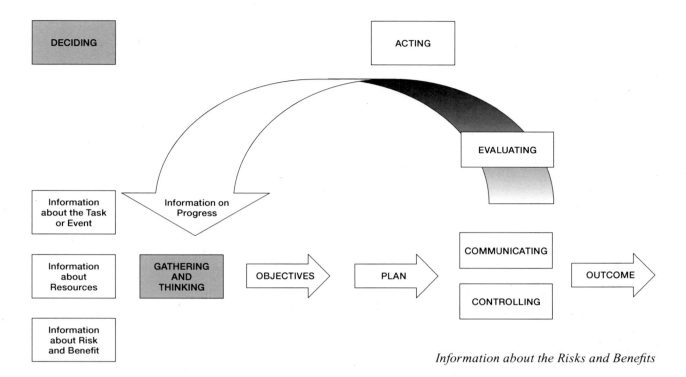

Information about the Risks and Benefits

6. Information about risk and benefit

6.1 In order to make a balanced decision it is essential that the potential risks are considered against perceived benefits.

6.2 In considering risk and benefit the broadest approach should be taken since they may apply to people, property, the environment or a combination of all of these and/or many others.

6.3 The Decision Maker should consider:

● Who and/or what is the event likely to present a risk to.
● What are the potential benefits from a particular course of action?

6.4 This will only become apparent when the process is applied to a specific task/event.

APPENDIX 4
Decision Making Model

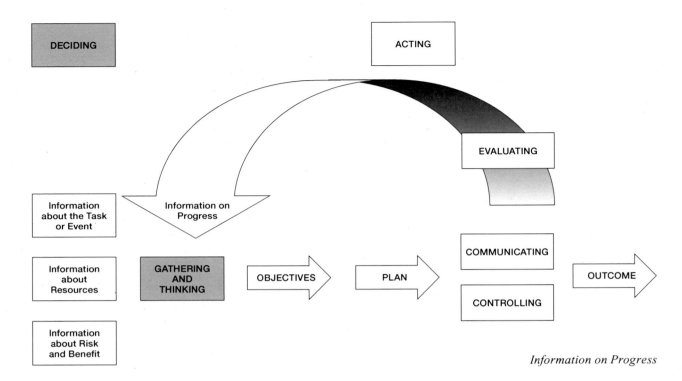

Information on Progress

7.   Information on Progress

7.1   As part of the process the Decision Maker will be presented with additional information as the situation develops. This information should be kept current from the very earliest stages.

7.2   At an early stage this information may be minimal, but as the event progresses the information will develop into a valuable source, shaping or changing the objectives and the overall plan.

7.3   As part of the cyclical nature of the Decision Making model, *Gathering Information on Progress* is considered in more detail later in this note.

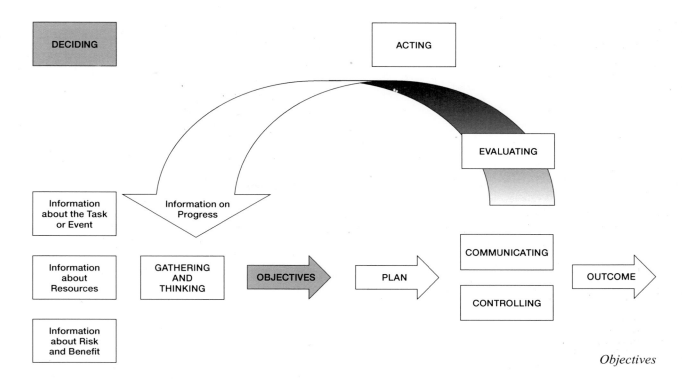

Objectives

8. Objectives

8.1   Once all the available information has been gathered and considered the Decision Maker will be able to identify and set a number of objectives that need to be achieved.

8.2   Clear and defined objectives give direction to resolve the task/event in a satisfactory manner thereby achieving the principle aim of the Authority: 'Making London a Safer City'

8.3   In setting detailed objectives the primary concern is the reduction of risk to people. Objectives that provide resolution to a static situation but expose members of the public or brigade to unnecessary risk would not therefore be acceptable.

8.4   The objectives and the plan subsequently developed to implement them should provide outcomes that are achievable with an acceptable level of risk for the situation.

8.5   It is therefore when setting the objectives that the link is made with Step 2 of the Dynamic Risk Assessment:

Select safe systems of work

APPENDIX 4
Decision Making Model

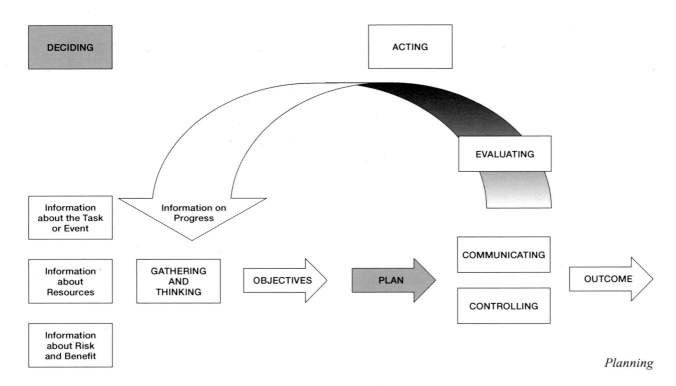

Planning

9. The Plan

9.1 This stage in the process requires that prioritised objectives be developed into plans that are achievable and take into account the need to reduce any risks to acceptable levels.

9.2 When developing effective plans, the achieving of set objectives is unlikely to be considered in isolation. There may be a number of conflicting priorities such as:

● Safety issues.
● Availability of resources
● Involvement of other agencies and their objectives.

9.3 All of these conflicting priorities need to be considered and accounted for in the plan. It is likely that the plan will set a number of primary objectives that, once achieved, can be built upon to achieve the final objectives.

9.4 The planning stage should result in the development of actions designed to deliver the required outcomes with an acceptable level of risk to those involved. These are defined as Safe Systems of Work.

9.5 Once the plan is developed the Decision Maker will need to make sure that sufficient resources are put into place to deliver it. This may relate to an individual obtaining a particular piece of equipment or the request by a Decision Maker for additional resources to deal with a developing situation.

9.6 Once the Plan has been formulated, the Decision Maker can move on to Step 3 of the Dynamic Risk Assessment:

Assess chosen systems of work
9.7 In a dynamic situation it is likely that plans will have to be modified as the situation develops.

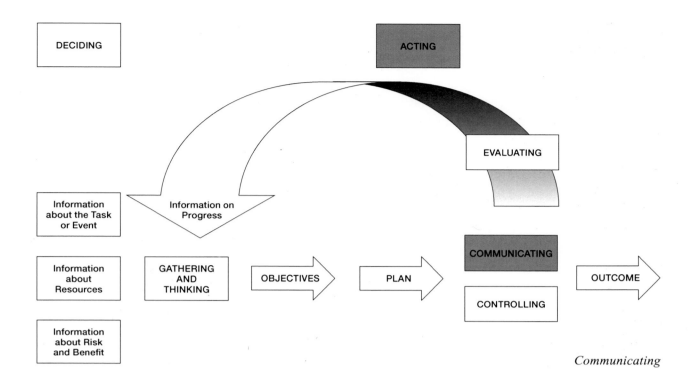

Communicating

10. Communicating

10.1   An essential element in the implementation of the plan is the need to ensure effective communication from and to the Decision Maker.

10.2   This is particularly relevant in dynamic situations where changes that are occurring may not be readily apparent to all those involved. Within this section of the model, key aspects exist that are essential to effective communication. These are:

● The Relevance of the information.
● The Accuracy of the information.
● The Timeliness of the information.
● Selection of the Medium to be used.

10.3   Effective communication will enable those involved to carry out their role in the plan and make sure that they are kept up to date with developments and progress. Communication must be two way to keep all parties updated on progress.

10.4   **Maintaining Relevance:** The information should be relevant to the recipient, as there may be little or no benefit from passing on all details of the event. Effectiveness of communication is often improved by only including details that affect the recipient, so keeping the information clear and concise. However, care should be taken not to exclude information that may indirectly affect individual efforts or safety, such as the work of others around them.

10.5   **Accuracy:** The information should be accurate to avoid confusion and misinterpretation when it is passed to the recipient. Good communication will leave the recipient in no doubt of what is expected.

10.6   **Timely information:** The information passed should be current. Information that is out dated or whose validity has expired should not be passed on.

10.7   **Choice of Medium:** When passing information it is important that a medium is used which is suitable to the situation. Examples of possible media include:

Verbal Communication, whether it be face to face or by radio.

● Visual Communications, such as Hand Signals.
● Written communication.

APPENDIX 4
Decision Making Model

10.8   The most appropriate medium will depend on the individual situation and the nature of the information to be passed. It would be inappropriate, for example, to rely on verbal communication in a noisy environment to pass a complex chemical name when a written note would avoid misinterpretation. The use of established communication routes and methods will assist in ensuring the effective flow of information to all those involved.

10.9   **Confirmation:** It is important to confirm that the communication has been received and understood. Often the easiest way to make sure that the recipient has accurately understood what is expected of them is to have them repeat it back.

11.   Controlling

11.1   Having communicated the plan to those involved it is necessary to make sure that resources are allocated appropriately, that the actions taken comply with the plan and safe systems of work are put into place. Responsibility for certain areas may be delegated to make sure control is maintained over the whole event and to enable individuals to carry out tasks effectively.

11.2   The degree to which the responsibility is delegated will depend on the complexity of the event and vary as it progresses. Delegation should aim at increasing rather than reducing the level of control the Decision Maker has over the event.

11.3   If the risks are not proportionate to the benefits of taking the action, additional control measures should be introduced. Here the link is made to Step 4 of the Dynamic Risk Assessment:

Introduce additional control measures

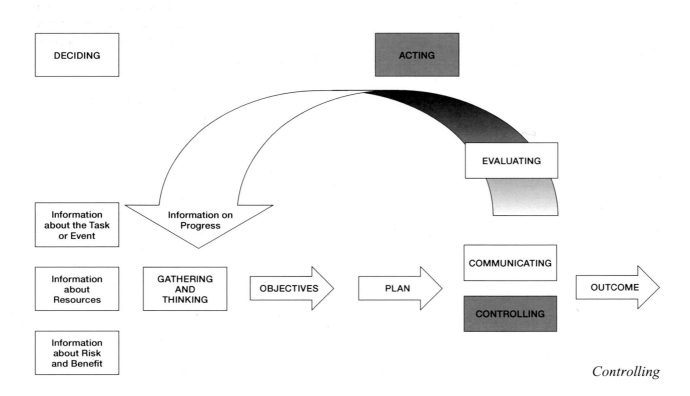

Controlling

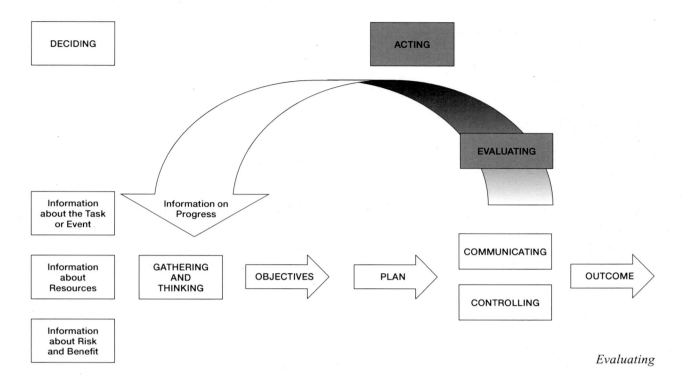

Evaluating

12. Evaluating

Seek/give progress and situation reports –

12.1   During the task/event the Decision Maker will receive information from a variety of sources. This will range from progress and situation reports to information gathered from the Decision Maker's own observations. All of this information can be used to assist the Decision Maker in evaluating the plan.

12.2   These reports should be provided regularly and it is the responsibility of all persons to pass these reports to the next level in the decision making chain.

12.3   It is the responsibility of the Decision Maker to make sure that all persons in the decision making chain are kept regularly informed of subsequent changes to the plan, the developing situation and progress being made. This process may relate to individuals carrying out tasks and providing feedback, or team leaders ensuring that team members are properly briefed.

12.4   At this stage it is also necessary to evaluate the systems of work and the effectiveness of any control measures. If the risk is still not proportionate to the benefits, then work should not proceed. This links with Step 5 of the Dynamic Risk Assessment:

Reassess systems of work and additional control measures.

APPENDIX 4
Decision Making Model

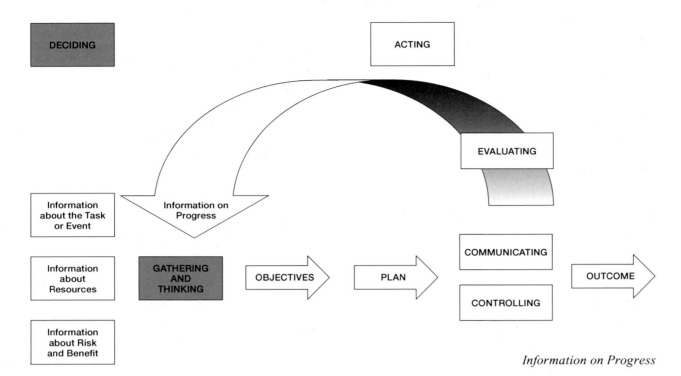

Information on Progress

13. Information on progress

13.1 As discussed earlier, Information on Progress will become of greater importance as the Acting elements of the Model are put in place.

13.2 It is at this stage that the Decision Making Model completes the loop and the first three elements along with the Information on Progress should be revisited.

Comparing progress made to that expected

13.3 Expected progress – Having formulated the plan and allocated the required resources with the relevant levels of control, the Decision Maker will have decided the timeframe within which objectives and events should be achieved. This is the expected progress to be made.

13.4 Actual progress – By receiving regular updates in the form of progress or situation reports the Decision Maker will be able to determine the actual progress being made.

13.5 Comparison – The Decision Maker will need to make a comparison between the progress expected against information on progress actually achieved. This will allow the Decision Maker to determine whether the plan is effective or requires amendment.

13.6 The results of the comparison between expectation and reality can then be used to supplement other information about the task/event in the 'Gathering and Thinking' part of the model. This additional information should then be considered and used by the Decision Maker to re-evaluate their objectives and plan.

13.7 The evaluation phase completes the information-gathering loop and ensures that the control of the task/event remains dynamic.

13.8 Whenever new information becomes available it is fed into the process and enables decision makers to make sure that the act of directing and controlling personnel and resources within an effective plan is based on all the available information.

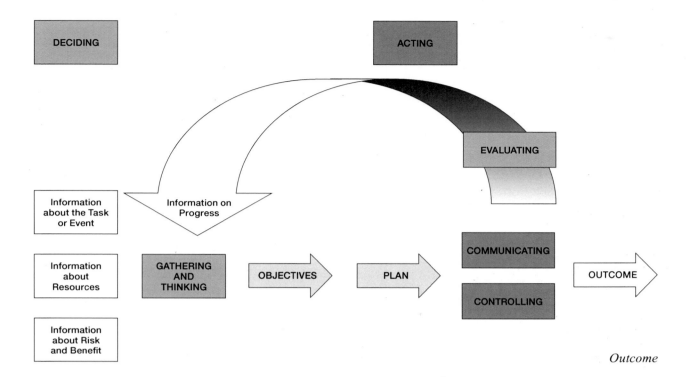

Outcome

14. Outcome

14.1   The outcome will be achieved successfully when the Objectives are met with minimal exposure to Risk.

14.2   On each occasion that new information, from any source, is introduced into the event the Decision Maker will evaluate the objectives, plan and control structure in light of this information, through use of the Decision Making Model, to ensure safe systems of work are maintained and resources are being used to best effect.

14.3   **Finally, it must be stressed that the use of the Decision Making Model should be continuous throughout an event. In the early dynamic stages it may be used many times and as the event becomes more controlled and less dynamic the model may be used less frequently.**

APPENDIX 5
Response Arrangements in Wales

Local response is the building block of resilience across the UK with operational response to emergencies being managed locally by the Strategic Co-ordination Groups (SCGs). The UK government and the Welsh Assembly Government work together on the development of civil protection policy. The concordat between UK Government and the Welsh Assembly Government on the Civil Contingencies Act 2004 provides clarity on the anticipated role(s) of the Welsh Assembly Government under this Act and, in particular relation to Emergency Powers under Part 2 of the Civil Contingencies Act 2004. The Welsh Assembly Government plays a vital role in the co-ordination of emergencies in or affecting Wales. Co-ordination arrangements in Wales are established to provide links and joint working protocols between multi-agency groups and organisations.

Welsh Assembly Government

The Assembly Government has devolved powers in agriculture; housing; education and training; the environment; health and health services; local government; and social services. It has responsibility for the front line public services of the Ambulance Service, NHS, Fire and Rescue Services. The Welsh Assembly Government, with its devolved powers, has an important role to play in terms political, social and economic aspects of the critical national infrastructure in Wales. In relation to this plan the Assembly Government will:

- Inform stakeholders of the activation of the pan-Wales Response Plan
- Set up an run the ECC(W)
- Act as Secretariat to the WCCC
- Establish links with COBR and the UK Government through the ECC(W)

Deploy Assembly Government Liaison Officers, where appropriate, to Strategic Co-ordination Groups.

The Wales Resilience Forum

The principal mechanism for multi-agency co-operation and co-ordination is the Wales Resilience Forum (WRF), which senior representation from the Welsh Assembly Government, Cabinet Office, local authorities, emergency services, armed forces, Environment Agency Wales, NHS Wales, Maritime and Coastguard Agency and the Health and Safety Executive.

The WRF is a planning body that considers resilience planning and preparation in a similar manner to the Regional Resilience Forums in England, but with a higher level of political involvement. The WRF works alongside other elements of the multi-agency protection framework at local and UK Government level. The framework is not a hierarchy; LRFs are not subordinate to the WRF, this allows for the free flow of information across the multi-agency structure.

The Wales Civil Contingencies Committee

The Wales Civil Contingencies Committee (WCCC) is constituted and functions in a similar way to the Regional Civil Contingencies Committees in England. The WCCC will be established for wide spread disruptive incidents requiring a pan Wales response and recovery effort. The membership of the WCCC will be determined by the nature of the incident and will be lead by a pre-determined lead official from a list of strategic officers and officials. The WCCC will not interfere with local command and control arrangements, but will ensure local responders are fully informed. The WCCC will meet at three levels:

Level 1 – prior to an emergency where warning is available. The meeting would be held to review the situation and update local stakeholders, with a view to escalating to Level Two if the situation warranted.

Level 2 – in the event of a wide area disruptive challenge in Wales. The meetings would be convened by the Welsh Assembly Government, in consultation with relevant members of the WRF. They might also be convened if a national response or national co-ordination of an event was required. The WCCC may also be convened for an emergency which occurs in Wales where the Strategic Co-ordinating Group or the WRF feels it will be able to add value to the response.

Level 3 – could only be called once an emergency arises which requires the making of emergency regulations under Part 2 of the Civil Contingencies Act.

The WCCC will request situation reports from local responders to ensure Welsh Ministers are fully briefed. Welsh Ministers will inevitably use this same information to brief UK Government Ministers, thus reducing the need for duplication.

The Emergency Co-ordination Centre Wales

When there is a requirement or expected escalation of an incident, the Welsh Assembly Government will activate the Emergency Co-ordination Centre Wales (ECC(W)). The ECC(W) provides an important role in the consequence management issues that arise from emergencies, particularly where the impact of those emergencies that affect devolved functions. The ECC(W) is a facility that supports the WCCC and Welsh Ministers in providing briefings and advice. Additionally, the EEC(W) provides a link between the SCGs, the office of the Secretary of State for Wales and Civil Contingencies Secretariat.

The primary role of the ECC(W) is to gather and disseminate information to Welsh Ministers and the UK government. Additionally, the ECC(W) will inform local SCGs of the pan UK picture ensuring good communication is maintained in order that local decisions reflect the needs of the UK.

The ECCW will assist in co-ordination of mutual aid/assistance and cross border issues during a major emergency, and where there are no established protocols in place the ECCW will assist in facilitation of a central link between UK Government departments and the devolved administrations. The decision to implement the ECC(W) will depend very much on the nature of the emergency in or affecting Wales.

Agencies that are not transferred functions will report directly to their respective UK department, although copy reports will be forwarded to the ECC(W) where appropriate.

In addition to their normal roles the Fire and Rescue Service will provide a representative as a liaison officer at the ECC(W) to act as a communication link between the ECC(W) and those Welsh Fire and Rescue Services involved. They will also provide situation and exceptional reports to the ECC(W) and link with the Welsh Assembly Government's Department for Social Justice and Regeneration on policy issues.

Under the provisions of the Civil Contingencies Act 2004 if emergency regulations are introduced that impact upon Wales the UK government will appoint a Wales Emergency Co-ordinator.

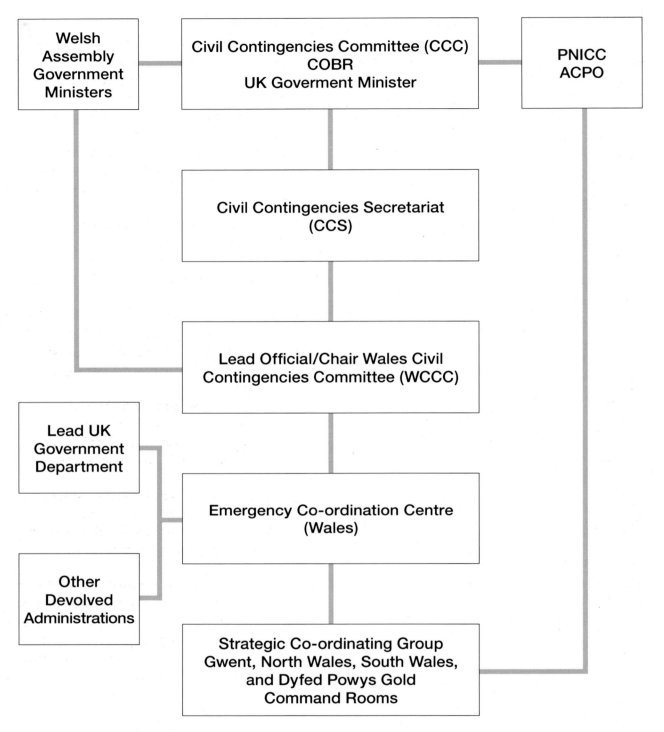

Co-ordination Arrangements and Communication Links in Wales

APPENDIX 6
Response Arrangements in Scotland

Local response is the building block of resilience across the UK with operational response to emergencies being managed locally by Strategic Co-ordinating Groups (SCGs). The UK government and the Scottish Executive work together on the development of civil protection policy. The Scottish Executive plays a vital role in the co-ordination of major emergencies in or affecting Scotland. Co-ordination arrangements in Scotland are established to provide links and joint working protocols between multi-agency groups and organisations.

Strategic Co-ordinating Groups

The principal mechanism for multi-agency co-operation and co-ordination across Scotland are the eight SCGs. SCGs are established in each police force area in Scotland and typically contain representation from the constituent local authorities, emergency services, armed forces, Scottish Environmental Protection Agency (SEPA), NHS, and the Maritime and Coastguard Agency (MCA). The SCGs consider resilience planning and preparation in a similar manner to the Regional Resilience Forums in England. They also participate in a Scotland – wide Strategic Co-ordinating Group Forum to facilitate information sharing, the development of good practice and promote consistency in preparation for response to emergencies in Scotland. The SCG (s) will be activated in the event of incidents requiring a strategic level of management.

The Lead Scottish Executive Department

Where the nature of the emergency is such that some degree of central government co-ordination or support becomes necessary, the Scottish Executive will consider designating a single Department to be responsible for its overall response to a significant emergency. The Scottish Executive will activate its corporate response arrangements to:

- act as the focal point for communication between the Scottish Executive, its sponsored bodies and the SCG(s);

- brief Ministers;
- produce a handling plan, as soon as possible, which offers a clear assessment of whether the emergency is within its scope or whether central co-ordination arrangements need to be invoked in consultation with Scottish Executive Justice Department;
- take whatever executive decisions and actions are needed from the centre to handle the emergency or to help local responders to deal with it;
- draw upon and apply resources to support the local response to the emergency;
- ensure effective liaison with UK Lead Government Departments regarding Scottish interests;
- co-ordinate and disseminate information for the public and the media at the national level;
- engage with stakeholder representatives at national level on matters of interest for Scotland;
- account to the Scottish Parliament and lead in the submission of evidence to any subsequent Government appointed inquiry;
- identify and share the lessons from the emergency;
- at all times assess whether the emergency remains within its scope or whether to activate the corporate Scottish Executive or UK central government arrangements.

If a single Department is nominated to lead it is likely that it will operate from its normal offices and, if necessary, provide direct input for SCGs. Once the Department recognises that the emergency has consequences for other Scottish Executive Departments it will activate SEER.

The Scottish Executive Emergency Room (SEER)

The precise role of SEER is likely to vary depending on the nature of the emergency at hand. SEER will not duplicate the role of local responders. It encompasses all Scottish Executive Departments and performs its role through a number of integrated groups, such as the Ministerial Group on Civil Contingencies (MGCC).

APPENDIX 6
Response Arrangements in Scotland

It will:

- provide strategic direction for Scotland;
- co-ordinate and support the activity of SE Departments;
- collate and maintain a strategic picture of the emergency response with a particular focus on consequence management and recovery issues;
- brief Ministers;
- identify if it is appropriate for a particular SE department to lead in a relevant area of response;
- ensure effective communication between local, Scottish and UK levels, including the co-ordination of reports on the response and recovery effort;
- mobilise Scottish assets and release them to support response and recovery efforts as appropriate;
- determine public information strategy and co-ordinate public advice in consultation with SCGs and other key stakeholders;
- advise on the relative priority to be attached to multi-site or multiple incidents and the allocation of scarce Scottish resources;
- co-ordinate and disseminate information for the public and the media at the national level;
- raise at UK level any issues that cannot be resolved in Scotland;

- ensure that UK strategies and input to response and recovery is co-ordinated with the Scottish and local efforts.

The Scottish Emergencies Co-ordinating Committee

The Scottish Emergencies Co-ordinating Committee (SECC) will provide support and advice to SEER in the event of a major emergency. The representation of agencies at SECC would be determined by the particular circumstances of the emergency. The role of the SECC is to provide specialist information and advice to support the development of Scotland's strategies.

UK Arrangements

When the particular circumstances of an emergency require co-ordination and support from U.K. Government, the Cabinet Office will consider instigating UK Government plans. When the decision to mobilise plans is made, links will be established with the Scottish Executive's corporate arrangements. The national structure for Managing Response is appended in Figure 1 overleaf.

N.B. (A full version of these arrangements can be found in "Preparing Scotland", available on the Scottish Executive website).

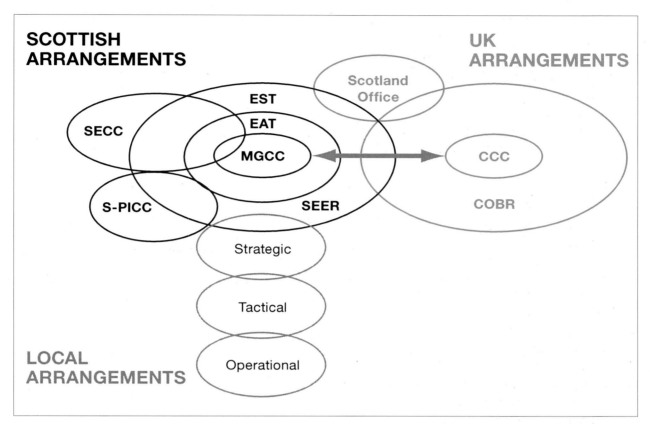

Figure 1

Key to Figure 1

MGCC – Ministerial Group on Civil Contingencies

SECC – Scottish Emergency Co-ordinating Committee

SCG – Strategic Co-ordinating Group

S-PICC – Scottish Police Information and Co-ordination Centre

SEER – Scottish Executive Emergency Room

EAT – Scottish Executive Emergency Action Team

EST – Scottish Executive Emergency Support Team

COBR – Cabinet Office Briefing Room

CCC – Civil Contingencies Committee

APPENDIX 7
Response Arrangements in Northern Ireland

The UK Government and the Northern Ireland Assembly work together on the development of Civil Protection Policy and ensure resilience at a local and National level.

The primary legislation in Northern Ireland relating to Fire and Rescue Services is 'The Fire and Rescue Services (Northern Ireland) Order 2006' with the 'Civil Contingencies Framework', the mechanism for discharging the principles of the Civil Contingencies Act 2004.

While Strategic Co-ordinating Groups (SCG's) provide a local response to UK resilience in England, Scotland and Wales, in Northern Ireland this role is carried out by the Crisis Management Group (CMG).

Crisis Management Group

The principal mechanism for multi-agency co-operation and co-ordination in Northern Ireland is the Crisis Management Group (CMG). This is chaired by the Head of the Northern Ireland Civil Service or the head of the Lead devolved government department as appropriate. Membership is made up of representatives of the nine devolved government departments. This group is supported at the planning and co-ordination of policy levels by the Emergency Services Senior Co-ordinating Group (ESSCG), comprising Fire, Police, Ambulance, Maritime and Coastguard Agency and Military and the Integrated Emergency Planning Forum (IEPF), made up of private and public sector major utility and transport organisations, who help co-ordinate and brief Category 2 responders in the event of a Regional/National emergency. Both of these forums participate in the sharing of information, the development of good practice and promote consistency in preparation and training in line with the principles of integrated emergency management. CMG will, in most instances, be activated in the event of incidents requiring a strategic level of management.

The Lead Department Principle

Where the nature of the emergency is such that some degree of central government co-ordination or support becomes necessary, the Northern Ireland Executive, in keeping with best practice, operate the lead Department principle. This in practice means that the nominated department who has overall responsibility for the type of emergency in progress will:

- act as the focal point for communication between the Northern Ireland Assembly, Northern Ireland Office (NIO) and the CMG/ESSCG;
- brief devolved administration Ministers and where necessary Northern Ireland Office (NIO) Ministers;
- take whatever executive decisions and actions are needed from the centre to handle the emergency or to help local responders to deal with it;
- draw upon and apply resources to support the local response to the emergency;
- ensure effective liaison with UK Lead Government Departments on all devolved matters;
- co-ordinate and disseminate information for the public and the media on devolved matters;
- engage with stakeholder representatives at national level on matters of interest for Northern Ireland on devolved matters;
- account to the Northern Ireland Assembly and lead in the submission of evidence to any subsequent Government appointed inquiry on all devolved matters;
- identify and share the lessons from the emergency;
- at all times assess whether the emergency remains within its scope or whether to activate UK central government arrangements.

The Northern Ireland Office Briefing Room (NIOBR)

NIOBR is the main communication link to Central Government and the other devolved regions. However, current governance arrangements mean that the Northern Ireland Office will act as the Lead Department for all terrorist related incidents. In effect this could mean that NIOBR will operate either in partnership or separate of the linkage with CMG (see Figure 1 Emergency Response Arrangements in Northern Ireland). Where NIOBR is established alongside CMG, it will not duplicate the role of local responders but support it at a strategic level and ensure links are established at National level with the Cabinet Office Briefing Room (COBR) or those of the other devolved regions. It encompasses all involved or effected government departments and is chaired by a NIO Minister.

It will:

- provide strategic direction on non devolved issues for Northern Ireland;
- support the activity of devolved Departments;
- collate and maintain a strategic picture of the emergency response with a particular focus on consequence management and recovery issues;
- brief Central Government Ministers on non devolved issues;
- ensure effective communication between the Northern Ireland Assembly and UK levels, including the co-ordination of reports on the response and recovery effort;

- determine public information strategy and co-ordinate public advice in consultation with the ESSCG and other key stakeholders on non devolved matters;
- advise on the relative priority to be attached to multi-site or multiple incidents and the allocation of resources on non devolved matters;
- co-ordinate and disseminate information for the public and the media at the national level on non devolved matters;
- raise at UK level any issues that cannot be resolved in Northern Ireland on non devolved matters;
- ensure that UK strategies and input to response and recovery is co-ordinated with the Northern Ireland Assembly efforts.
- determine public information strategy and co-ordinate public advice in consultation with the ESSCG and other key stakeholders on non devolved matters;
- advise on the relative priority to be attached to multi-site or multiple incidents and the allocation of resources on non devolved matters;
- co-ordinate and disseminate information for the public and the media at the national level on non devolved matters;
- raise at UK level any issues that cannot be resolved in Northern Ireland on non devolved matters;
- ensure that UK strategies and input to response and recovery is co-ordinated with the Northern Ireland Assembly efforts.

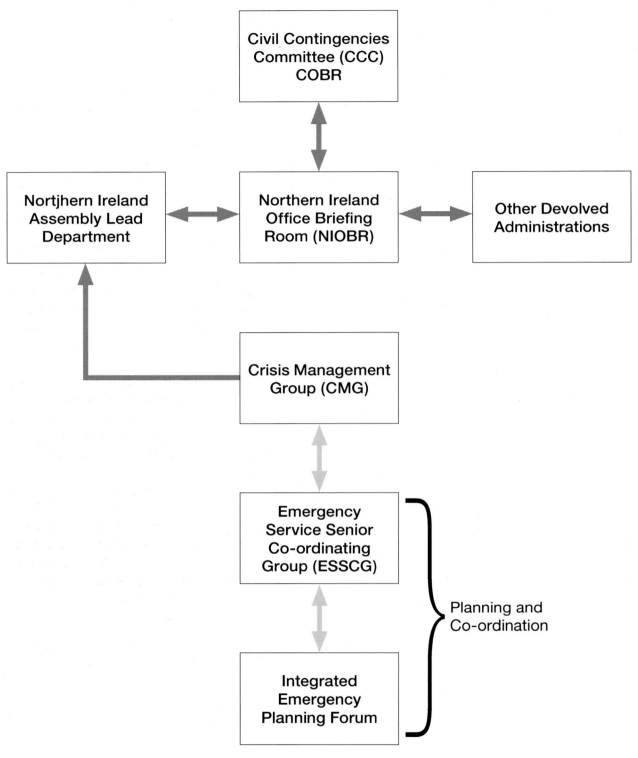

Communication Link Key

Planning and/or co-ordination

In emergency situation

Emergency Response Arrangements in Northern Ireland

Glossary of Terms

ANALYTICAL RISK ASSESSMENT (ARA)– having carried out a DRA and established a Tactical Mode, the IC will be aware of the hazards, the people at risk and the necessary control measures to protect those at risk. This initial assessment forms the basis of a more detailed risk assessment which in the FRS is termed the Analytical Risk Assessment.

BRIDGEHEAD – a central and advanced control point for occasions where it is necessary for BA to be started up at a distance from the original point of entry to a risk area, whilst remaining in a safe air environment (TB 1/97).

COMMAND – the authority for an agency to direct the actions of its own resources (both personnel and equipment).

COMMAND LINE – the line or chain of command at an incident. The ICS relies upon a single unified command line. With the exception of urgent safety related issues officers should not take control of operations outside their assigned responsibility and should ensure all information and instruction is passed via the relevant command line officers.

COMMAND POINT – point from which Incident Commander operates, this may be a car, appliance, specialist unit or part of a building.

COMMAND SUPPORT – Command Support is a role undertaken by one or more staff at an incident. The role typically provides recording, liaison, detailed resource management and information gathering for the Incident Commander. At large incidents Command Support may comprise a dedicated team working from a mobile command unit and may include individuals tasked with supporting Sector Commanders. However, Command Support is not directly in the command line.

COMMAND TEAM – the ICS relies on shared responsibility and authority. While the Incident Commander retains overall responsibility for the incident, and dictates the overall tactical plan, the decision making for, and control of, local operations is kept as close as possible to those operations. This is achieved by the creation of a single command line from the crew commander to the Incident Commander. This command line, together with staff tasked with supporting commanders, is the Command Team. For ICS purposes the Command Team is usually taken to be the Incident Commander, Operations Commander(s) and Sector Commanders, together with Command Support staff.

CONTACT POINT – a designated point (usually an appliance not involved in operations or an officer's car) from which a nominated member of personnel will carry out the Command Support function at a small to medium size incident.

CONTROL – the authority to direct strategic and tactical operations in order to complete an assigned function and includes, where agreed, the ability to direct the activities of other agencies engaged in the completion of that function. The control of an assigned function also carries with it a responsibility for the health and safety of those involved.

CREW MANAGER – an officer tasked with supervising specific tasks or meeting specific objectives utilising one or more fire-fighters.

DYNAMIC RISK ASSESSMENT (DRA) – this is the continuous assessment of risk in the rapidly changing circumstances of an operational incident, which is done in order to implement the control measures necessary to ensure an acceptable level of safety. Dynamic Risk Assessment (DRA) is particularly appropriate during the time critical phase of an incident, which is usually typical of the arrival and escalation phase of an incident, but at the earliest opportunity the Dynamic Risk Assessment should be supported by analytical risk assessment.

COMMUNITIES AND LOCAL GOVERN-MENT EMERGENCY ROOM (FIRE AND RESCUE) – an advisory group established by the Chief Fire and Rescue Advisor to support the Director of Fire and Resilience and the fire minister during serious incidents.

ENHANCED COMMAND SUPPORT (ECS) – a communications and co-ordination facility to support operations during incidents requiring national mobilisation and use of strategic holding areas.

FORWARD COMMAND POST – point, near the scene of operations, where the officer delegated responsibility for command in that area is sited. This may be at a bridgehead.

GENERIC RISK ASSESSMENT – risk assessments that have been produced to assist the FRS with their regulatory requirements and published in "Volume 3 – A Guide to Operational Risk Assessment".

INCIDENT COMMANDER – the nominated competent officer having overall responsibility for dictating tactics and resource management.

INNER CORDON – a secured area which surrounds the immediate site of the incident and provides security for it. Such an area will typically have some formal means of access control. This surrounds the immediate scene and provides security for it.

INTER AGENCY LIAISON OFFICER (ILO) – a trained and qualified officer who can advise and support Incident Commanders, Police, Medical, Military and other Government Agencies on the organisations operational capacity and capability to reduce risk and safely resolve incidents at where an attendance may be required. This will include major incidents, public order, domestic or any other situation that would benefit from the attendance of the ILO.

MARSHALLING AREA – area to which resources not immediately required at the scene or being held for future use can be directed to standby. May be a sector function under a Marshalling Sector Commander, reporting to Incident Commander via Command Support.

NATIONAL CO-ORDINATION CENTRE (FRS NCC) – a facility established to co-ordinate the mobilisation of national resources such as USAR teams, mass decontamination units, DIM vehicles etc when needed.

OPERATIONS COMMANDER – an officer tasked with co-ordinating and directing the operations of several sectors. Responsible directly to the Incident Commander. When an Operations Commander is assigned, operational Sector Commanders will report to the Operations Commander rather than the Incident Commander. Assigning an Operations Commander at an incident which has several operational sectors keeps the span of control of the Incident Commander to be maintained at a satisfactory level.

OUTER CORDON – an area which surrounds the inner cordon and seals off a wider area of the incident from the public. This designates the controlled area into which unauthorised persons are not permitted access. It encompasses the inner cordon, and the area between into which command positions and other essential activities (such as post-decontamination casualty management) are set up.

RENDEZVOUS POINT (RVP)- point to which all resources at the scene are initially directed for logging, briefing and deployment.

RISK ASSESSMENT – a risk assessment involves an identification of hazards, and an estimation of the risks, taking into account the existing precautions available and used, and a consideration of what else needs to be done.

SAFETY – a state where exposure to hazards has been controlled to an acceptable level.

SAFETY OFFICER – officer delegated specific responsibility for monitoring operations and ensuring safety of personnel working on the incident ground or a designated section of it.

SAFE SYSTEMS OF WORK – a formal procedure which results from systematic examination of a task in order to identify all the hazards and risks posed. It defines safe methods to ensure that hazards are eliminated or risks controlled as far as possible.

SECTOR – a sector is the area of responsibility of a Sector Commander (i.e. a sector should not be created unless someone is given the responsibility for running it.) Sectors should be created to manage spans of control and provide tighter supervision of operations. Boundaries between geographic sectors may be geographic features, walls, roads differences in elevation or separate areas of plant. Operational sectors are those dealing directly with the incident, typically operational sectors will undertake fire fighting, rescue, cooling and so on. Support sectors are those not dealing directly with the incident. Support sectors are usually defined by the function they undertake, for instance decontamination, foam supply, marshalling or water supply.

SECTOR COMMANDER – an officer commanding a sector, who is tasked with responsibility for tactical and safety management of a clearly identified part of an incident. Subject to objectives set by the Incident Commander the Sector Commander has control of all operations within the sector and must remain within it.

SPAN OF CONTROL – the number of lines of communication that a single individual has to maintain. This is usually defined by the number of people who potentially require an officer's attention for briefing, reporting, passing instructions or other incident management concerns, in order to carry out their role at the incident. As a guide five such reporting lines are considered the usual optimum for an Incident Commander to maintain during an incident. This may be increased at an incident, which is well in hand or have to be reduced to two or three during the early stages of a rapidly escalating or highly complex incident. Management of the Span of Control must be effective throughout the command line.

STRATEGIC HOLDING AREA (SHA) – a key location that has been identified on a motorway or trunk road as a suitable space to accommodate FRS resources and national assets in response to a major incident.

STRATEGY – in the context of incident command, this is the highest level of planning for dealing with situations either in advance of an incident or while incidents are underway (sometimes called "Gold Command").

TACTICS – the deployment of personnel and equipment on the incident ground to achieve the aims of the strategic plan.

References and Bibliography

Adamson. A. (1970) The Effective Leader. Pitman.

Bonney, J. (1995) Fire command teams: what makes for effective performance? Fire Service College, Brigade Command Course Project 2/95.

Brunacini, A. (2002) Fire Command (2nd Ed) Quincy, Mass. National Fire Protection Association. ISBN 0-87765-500-6

Burke, E. (1997) Competence in command: Research and development in the London Fire Brigade. In R. Flin, E. Salas, M. Strub & L. Martin (Eds) Decision Making under Stress. Aldershot: Ashgate.

Cannon-Bowers, J., Tannenbaum, S., Salas, E. & Volpe, C. (1995) Defining Competencies and establishing team training requirements. In R. Guzzo & E. Salas (Eds.) Team Effectiveness and Decision Making in Organisations. San Francisco: Jossey Bass.

Charlton, D. (1992, April) Training and assessing submarine commanders on the Perishers' course. In collected papers of the First Offshore Installation Management Conference: Emergency Command Responsibilities. Robert Gordon University, Aberdeen.

Driskell, J. & Salas, E. (1996) (Eds) Stress and Human Performance. Mahwah, NJ: LEA.

Flin, R. (1995) Incident command: Decision making and team work. Journal of the Fire Service College, 1, 7-15.

Flin, R. (1995) Crew Resource Management for teams in the offshore oil industry. Journal of European Industrial Training, 19.9, 23-27.

Flin, R. (1996) Sitting in the Hot Seat. Leaders and Teams for Critical Incident Management. Chichester: Wiley.

Flin R, Arbuthnot K (Eds) (2002) *Incident Command: Tales from the Hotseat*, Aldershot, Ashgate.

Flin, R., Salas, E., Strub, M. & Martin, L. (1997) (Eds) Decision Making under Stress: Emerging Themes and Applications. Aldershot: Ashgate.

Fredholm, L. (1997) Decision making patterns in major fire-fighting and rescue operations. In R. Flin, E. Salas, M. Strub & L. Martin (Eds) Decision Making under Stress. Aldershot: Ashgate.

HM Govt, (2005), Emergency Preparedness, Cabinet Office. www.ukresilience.info/preparedness.aspx

HM Govt, (2005), Emergency Response and Recovery. www.ukresilience.info/response.aspx

Keampf, G. & Militello, L. (1992) The Problem of Decision Making in Emergencies. Fire International No 135, p 38-39.

Kerstholt, J.H. (1997) Dynamic decision making in non-routine situations, in R.Flin, E Salas, M. Strub, & L. Martin, Decision making under stress. Ashgate, Aldershot, UK.

Kissinger, H; 1982, "Years of Upheaval", Boston, Little Brown

Klein, G. (1998) Sources of Power How People Make Decisions. Cambridge, Mass: MIT Press.

Klein, G. (1997) The Recognition-Primed Decision (RPD) model: Looking back, looking forward. In C. Zsambok & G. Klein (Eds) Naturalistic Decision Making. Mahwah, NJ: Lawrence Erlbaum.

Klein, G., Calderwood, R., & Clinton-Cirocco, A. (1986) Rapid decision making on the fireground. In Proceedings of the Human Factors Society 30th Annual Meeting. San Diego: HFS.

Klein, G., Orasanu, J., Calderwood, R. & Zsambok, C. (1993). (Eds.) Decision Making in Action. New York: Ablex.

Murray, B. (1994) More guidance needed for senior commanders on the fireground. Fire, 87, June, 21-22.

Orasanu, J. (1995) Training for aviation decision making: the naturalistic decision making perspective. Proceedings of the Human Factors and Ergonomics Society 39th annual Meeting. San Diego, Santa Monica CA: The Human Factors and Ergonomics Society.

Orasanu, J. & Fischer, U. (1997) Finding decisions in naturalistic environments: The view from the cockpit. In C. Zsambok & G. Klein (Eds) Naturalistic Decision Making. Mahwah, NJ: LEA.

Salas, B., Bowers, C. & Edens, B. (in press) (eds.) Applying Resource Management in Organisations. New Jersey. LEA.

Schmitt, J. (1994) Mastering Tactics. Tactical Decision Game Workbook. Quantico, Virginia. US Marine Corps Association.

Wynne, D. (1995) Expert teams performing in natural environments. Fire Service College, Brigade Command Course Project 1/95.

Zsambok, C. & Klein, G. (1997) (Eds) Naturalistic Decision Making. Mahwah, NJ: LEA.

Further Reading

Fire Service Guides to Risk Assessment

Volume 1 – A Guide for Senior Officers
ISBN 0 11 341218 5

Volume 2 – A Guide for Fire Service Managers
ISBN 0 11 3412193

Volume 3 – A Guide to Operational Risk
Assessment
ISBN 0 11 3412207

Acknowledgements

As editor of the 3rd Edition of the FRS manual on incident command I would like to record my appreciation and gratitude to a number of individuals and groups who contributed to the production of it. There were many consultees and contributors, but the following deserve mention.

Fire Service College:

Dave Newman who undertook the major task of assembling the copy, liaising with consultees and generally managing the process of pulling the project of producing the 3rd edition together. Brian Taylor who lead the contribution on competence and members of the incident management team. The staff of the Centre for Leadership who were instrumental in developing the leadership doctrine component, and Bridgette Schneider-Brown who devoted many hours to detailed proof-reading. Keith Phillipson who kindly refreshed and reproduced all diagrams other than those acknowledged as being from other sources.

West Yorkshire Fire and Rescue Service

Thanks to CFO Phil Toase CBE and many of his staff for permission to use the foundation work developed in that authority which has been carried over from Editions One and Two which were authored by West Yorkshire, and specific acknowledgement to the contributions of Ian Gilchrist, Dave Turner, Steve Woodfield and Phil Langdale.

CFOA

Operations Committee and its command and control sub-committee, the National Command and Control Co-ordination Group (NCCCG) who considered a series of drafts, made useful observations and contributions throughout and approved the draft. Richard Haigh of Grampian FRS, Louis Jones of Northern Ireland FRS and Steve Skivens of South Wales FRS for the appendices contextualising the UK resilience framework to the devolved administrations.

Communities and Local Government Fire and Resilience Directorate and Chief Fire and Rescue Adviser's Unit

All who contributed to policy development, risk management policy development and final production, including Health and Safety, IPDS and New Dimension input.

Health and Safety Executive

For detailed critique of Chapter 4.

Photographs

Thanks to the following FRSs for permission to use photographs: West Yorkshire FRS; West Midlands FRS; London FB; Hertfordshire FRS; Strathclyde FRS; The Fire Service College.

Kevin Arbuthnot QFSM
The Fire Service College
And CFOA lead on Incident Command.

Editor and co-author of the 3rd Edition;
August 2007.

Notes